BIBLE

Student Edition • Grade 3

Colorado Springs, Colorado

© 2012 by ACSI/Purposeful Design Publications

All rights reserved. No portion of this book may be reproduced, stored in a retrieval system, or transmitted, in any form or by any means—mechanical, photocopying, recording, or otherwise—without prior written permission of ACSI/Purposeful Design Publications.

Purposeful Design Publications is the publishing division of the Association of Christian Schools International (ACSI) and is committed to the ministry of Christian school education, to enable Christian educators and schools worldwide to effectively prepare students for life. As the publisher of textbooks, trade books, and other educational resources within ACSI, Purposeful Design Publications strives to produce biblically sound materials that reflect Christian scholarship and stewardship and that address the identified needs of Christian schools around the world.

References to books, computer software, and other ancillary resources in this series are not endorsements by ACSI. These materials were selected to provide teachers with additional resources appropriate to the concepts being taught and to promote student understanding and enjoyment.

Unless otherwise identified, all Scripture quotations are taken from the Holy Bible, New King James Version (NKJV), © 1982 by Thomas Nelson, Inc. Used by permission. All rights reserved.

Printed in the United States of America
18 17 16 15 14 13 12   1 2 3 4 5 6 7

Elementary Bible, grade 3
Purposeful Design Elementary Bible series
ISBN 978-1-58331-258-2   Student edition   Catalog #10031

Purposeful Design Publications
A Division of ACSI
PO Box 65130 • Colorado Springs, CO 80962-5130
Customer Service: 800-367-0798 • www.purposefuldesign.com

Table of Contents

Lesson 1 Jesus in the Beginning 1

Lesson 2 Jesus' Birth and Childhood 5

Lesson 3 Jesus Prepares for Ministry 9

Lesson 4 The First Four Disciples 13

Lesson 5 Equipping the Disciples 17

Lesson 6 The Beatitudes 21

Lesson 7 Building on the Rock 25

Lesson 8 "I Am" Statements 29

Lesson 9 The Lord's Prayer 33

Lesson 10 Walking in Love 37

Lesson 11 Born Again 41

Lesson 12 Responding to the Gospel 45

Lesson 13 Thanksgiving 49

Lesson 14 Seeking the Lost 53

Lesson 15 Forgiving 57

Lesson 16 Stewardship 61

Lesson 17 Christmas 65

Lesson 18 Jesus' First Miracle 69

Lesson 19	Jesus Satisfies	73
Lesson 20	Walking on Water	77
Lesson 21	Healing a Blind Man	81
Lesson 22	Lazarus Lives	85
Lesson 23	The Transfiguration	89
Lesson 24	The Holy Spirit	93
Lesson 25	Peter Is Transformed	97
Lesson 26	Stephen and the Early Church	101
Lesson 27	Saul's Conversion	105
Lesson 28	Paul's Early Ministry	109
Lesson 29	Easter	113
Lesson 30	Paul's First Two Missionary Journeys	117
Lesson 31	Paul's Third Journey	121
Lesson 32	Paul's Journey to Rome	125
Lesson 33	The Great Commission	129
Lesson 34	Review	133
Glossary		137

Name _____

Jesus in the Beginning 1.1

Welcome to third-grade Bible! This year you will learn many exciting things about the life of Jesus, God's Son, and the early Church.

God the Father, God the Son, and God the Holy Spirit are not three separate Gods. They are one God in three Persons. They are known as **the Trinity**.

Quality	Meaning
omnipotent	all-powerful
omnipresent	always present
omniscient	all-knowing

God has certain qualities that no person has. These qualities describe who He is and what He can do. Look at the chart to learn three of God's qualities.

Use your Glossary to fill in the blanks with the correct answers: **the Trinity**, omnipotent, omnipresent, omniscient.

1. God is all-powerful, or _____.

   God knows everything. He is _____.

   God is everywhere, all at the same time. He is

   _____.

   Together God the Father, God the Son, and God the Holy Spirit are called

   _____.

Use the words from the blanks to write the word each verse is describing.

2. Genesis 1:1 _____

3. Genesis 1:2 _____

4. Genesis 1:26 _____

1.2 Jesus in the Beginning

Jesus was in the beginning with God. He is God's Son. Because Jesus is God, He is eternal. He has always been and always will be.

Jesus became flesh. That means He came to live on the earth as a human being. Jesus was fully God and fully man. He came to show people what God the Father is like and to make a way for people to know God.

People were confused and lost because of sin. They were separated from God—like being all alone in a dark room. In a very special way, Jesus was life and light. God sent Jesus to light up that darkness and to show people the way to know Him.

Even though Jesus had created everything in the world, many people thought He was just an ordinary man. Those who really believed that Jesus is God became sons and daughters of God—and you can too. He offers salvation and eternal life to everyone who believes in Him.

1. Check the phrases that correctly complete the sentence:

When Jesus became flesh, He ____.

____ was hungry ____ was sinless ____ was able to feel pain

____ was tired ____ was tempted ____ was able to experience death

Read Galatians 4:4–5, and answer the questions.

2. What was Jesus sent to do?

_____.

3. What benefit could people receive from His coming?

_____.

Name _____

Jesus in the Beginning 1.3

Read and answer the questions.

1. At a friend's house last summer, Hailey decided to become a follower of Jesus. She was very happy about this decision, but when she returned home, things became very hard. Hailey's parents do not have a relationship with Jesus. They do not go to church or read the Bible. Hailey does not know how she can learn more about Jesus. Read Philippians 1:6. According to this verse, what can Hailey count on God to do for her?

_____

_____

2. Kai and Logan are best friends. They wear the same kind of shoes and like the same sports. There is one thing that is not the same. Kai knows that Jesus is the Son of God and that He died for people's sins, but Logan does not know this. Every time Kai mentions anything about Jesus, Logan changes the subject. Read Romans 1:16. On the basis of this verse, should Kai stop sharing about Jesus? Why or why not?

_____

_____

Both Hailey and Kai can grow in their faith by reading their Bible. Kai can use his Bible to share the plan of salvation. Unscramble the letters to complete the sentences. Use the Bible verses for clues.

3. God wants believers to grow in _____. (Luke 17:5)

THFAI

4. God wants believers to be _____ for Him. (Acts 1:8)

NESSESWIT

1.4 Jesus in the Beginning

It is helpful to know how the Bible is organized. Then you can quickly find what you are looking for. Use the Word Bank to label the different sections of the Bible.

WORD BANK
Prophecy
History
Gospels
History and Letters
Poetry
Law
Prophets

Old Testament

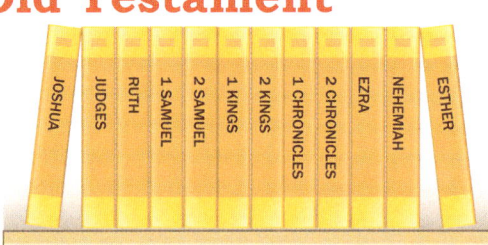

1. _____   2. _____

3. _____   4. _____

New Testament

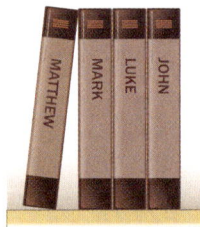

5. _____

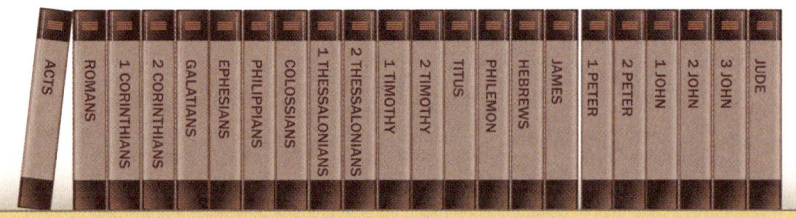

6. _____

7. _____

Name _____

Jesus' Birth and Childhood 2.1

Read the Scriptures. Use the Word Bank, and write the name of who is being described in each box. Circle each answer that shows someone who received a **revelation** from God about Jesus' birth.

WORD BANK
Mary
Joseph
Gabriel
Elizabeth
shepherds
wise men

1. They visited Jesus after an angel told them to find Him in a manger. _____
(Luke 2:8–12)

2. An angel told him Mary was going to have a son through the Holy Spirit. _____
(Matthew 1:20–21)

3. He told Mary she would have God's Son and she was to name Him Jesus. _____
(Luke 1:26–27 and 1:31)

4. They came to give Jesus gifts after seeing His star in the sky.
_____
(Matthew 2:1 and 2:9–11)

5. The baby inside this woman leaped when he heard Mary's greeting.
_____
(Luke 1:41)

6. She was Jesus' mother and praised God.
_____
(Luke 1:30 and 1:46)

Bible Grade 3

2.2 Jesus' Birth and Childhood

1. Sequence the order of events, listing them in order 1–6. Then illustrate one of the sentences.

   _____ Jesus stays and talks with the teachers in Jerusalem.

   _____ Jesus' parents find Him in the temple.

   _____ Mary and Joseph look for Jesus among the travelers.

   _____ Mary and Joseph travel without Jesus.

   _____ Jesus returns with His parents to go home.

   _____ Mary and Joseph return to Jerusalem.

2. Write the definition of divine.

   _____

   _____

Jesus' Birth and Childhood 2.3

Luke 2:52 says that Jesus grew in wisdom and stature. That means He acted wisely year after year. He learned new things and then made good decisions based on what He had learned. Read Proverbs 30:24–28. Think about each animal mentioned. Choose a word from the Word Bank that best describes how each animal represents wisdom.

WORD BANK
helpful
united
prepared
resourceful

1. Ants are small. They have food in the winter because they gather it in the summer. The ants are wise because they are _____.

2. Rock badgers are also known as coneys or shephanim. They live in rock formations. They search for food together. Some rock badgers act as guards and warn the others of danger. The rock badgers are wise because they are _____ to one another.

3. Locusts do not have a leader, yet they swarm together and fly great distances. The swarm of locusts then eats the crops where they land. Locusts are wise because they are _____ in what they do.

4. Spiders and lizards are both animals you can easily catch. They are common, yet they live in wealthy palaces. Spiders and lizards are wise because they are _____. This means they use what is available to them.

5. Use one of the four words from the Word Bank to describe a time when you acted wisely. _____
_____

2.4 Jesus' Birth and Childhood

Finish these sentences to indicate how you can grow in each of the following areas:

1. I can grow in **wisdom** by _____

   _____.

2. I can grow **physically** by _____

   _____.

3. I can grow **spiritually** by _____

   _____.

4. I can grow **socially** by _____

   _____.

Which of the following three areas do you need to grow in the most right now and why: in wisdom, in relationship to God (spiritually), or in relationship to people (socially)?

5. _____

   _____

   _____

   _____

   _____

   _____

Jesus talks to the teachers in the temple.

Name _____

Jesus Prepares for Ministry 3.1

1. Look up the word <mark>ministry</mark> in the Glossary. Write the definition on the lines.

_____

_____

2. Draw a line from each job to a description of how to prepare for that job. Then write how a person could use each job as an opportunity for ministry.

Preparation	Job	Ministry
study how to design buildings •	• Doctor	_____ _____
study life saving and get in good physical shape •	• Teacher	_____ _____
study about medicine •	• Fireman	_____ _____
study about education •	• Architect	_____ _____

© Bible Grade 3

3.2 Jesus Prepares for Ministry

Remember that John the Baptist came to prepare the way for Jesus. John preached to the people to confess and repent of their sins. He baptized people as a symbol of repentance. He also told people about Jesus. Look up the verses. Write what John revealed to the people about Jesus.

1. Matthew 3:11

_____

_____

2. John 1:29

_____

_____

3. John 1:34

_____

_____

4. Read Matthew 3:13–17. In the box below, draw a picture of Jesus' baptism.

Name _____

Jesus Prepares for Ministry

Before Jesus began His years of ministry, Satan tempted Him in three ways. Jesus resisted these temptations by quoting Scriptures. You can resist Satan by doing exactly as Jesus did!

1. Read Matthew 4:1–11. Fill in the chart about the three temptations, and read Jesus' response.

The Temptation	Jesus' Response
Verse 3 Satan told Jesus to … _____ _____ .	**Verse 4** Jesus met His spiritual needs by thinking about and believing the words of God.
Verses 5–6 Satan took Jesus to the highest point of the temple, and said … _____ _____ .	**Verse 7** Jesus quoted Scripture to resist Satan and to show that Satan was using Scripture incorrectly.
Verses 8–9 Satan took Jesus to a high mountain and said … _____ _____ .	**Verse 10** Jesus worshipped only God.

2. Write the definition of <mark>temptation</mark> on the lines.

_____

_____

3.4 Jesus Prepares for Ministry

Each of the students below faces a tempting situation. Just like Jesus, they can use the Sword of the Spirit, the Bible, to fight against the urge to do wrong. They need help in knowing where to find the verses that speak about their exact problems. Read each exercise. Then look up the three verses listed below. Write the letter of the verse that best fits in each situation.

    a. Ephesians 4:25   **b. James 4:11**   **c. Philippians 2:2–4**

1. Charita felt bad for Kari because Kari did not do well in her schoolwork. Kari was shy, and she stuttered. She dressed differently too. Charita was having a slumber party for her ninth birthday, and she really felt she should invite Kari. But what would the other kids think?

   _____

2. Ben's mom had promised to take him and his friends out for pizza if he got an A on his next math test. Ben thought he did really well on the test; but when the tests were handed back, he found he had scored a B+. Ben was tempted to lie: "What if I say I lost my test on the way home?"

   _____

3. Jenni had been watching Shannon. Shannon always got good grades, and her artwork was always hanging up outside the classroom. "Does she ever do anything wrong?" wondered Jenni. Then Jenni spotted Shannon laughing with some other kids. Jenni turned to her friends and said, "Who does she think she is? Does she think she's perfect?

   _____

Name _____

The First Four Disciples 4.1

1. Draw a line to match the disciple to the description about him.

Peter •   • brother of James

Andrew •   • brother of Peter

John •   • also called Simon

James •   • brother of John

2. Describe how these disciples might have felt when they heard Jesus say, "Follow me."

_____

_____

3. What did these disciples do to obey Jesus?

_____

_____

4. What would you give up if Jesus asked you to follow Him like He asked the disciples? Use the word respond in your answer.

_____

_____

4.2 The First Four Disciples

1. The disciples heard Jesus' voice call them. What are some ways you can hear God speaking to you?

_____

_____

2. In each circle below, draw one picture of something the disciples had to leave behind when they followed Jesus (Mark 6:8–9).

3. Circle the words that describe how you should respond to God.

obey   wait   trust   ask others if you should obey

immediately respond   listen   make excuses

worry   pray for courage to obey

4. When you listen to and obey God, what does that tell Him about you?

_____

_____

_____

Name _____

The First Four Disciples 4.3

1. Where can you be a fisher of men? Write the names of places you go and groups you belong to on the fish around the page.

2. Fill in the grid to show the differences between being a fisher of men in Jesus' time and being one now.

	Disciples	Me
Methods of travel		
Methods used to tell people about Jesus		
Help came from . . .		

3. Write two ways God equips believers today.

   a. _____

   b. _____

4. Color in the scale from left to right, stopping at the place that shows how equipped you feel to tell people about Jesus.

0 low   10 high

© Bible Grade 3

4.4 The First Four Disciples

Read the verses at the end of each sentence. Then write the words from the Word Bank to complete the sentences.

WORD BANK
Patmos
Peter
killed
healed
letters
pray

1. When _____ preached to the crowd, God added about 3,000 believers. (Acts 2:37–41)

2. God _____ a lame or crippled man after Peter spoke in the name of Jesus. (Acts 3:1–7)

3. The disciples asked Jesus to teach them how to _____. (Luke 11:1–4)

4. John was sent to the island of _____ because he preached the gospel, the good news about Jesus. (Revelation 1:9)

5. John wrote _____ to other believers so that they would know they had eternal life. (1 John 5:13)

6. James was _____ for telling others the good news about Jesus. (Acts 12:1–2)

Write a complete sentence to answer the question.

7. God worked in the disciples' lives as they grew in their faith in Christ. How is God working in your life as you grow in your faith?

_____

_____

_____

Name _____

Equipping the Disciples | 5.1

1. Write the names of the 12 disciples (Mark 3:16–19). They listened to God and walked in **fellowship** together.

P _____   M _____

J _____   T _____

J _____   J _____

A _____   T _____

P _____   S _____

B _____   J _____

2. Draw some of the 12 disciples in fellowship with Jesus.

5.2 Equipping the Disciples

After Jesus went back to heaven, God gave power to the disciples through the Holy Spirit. This power helped equip them to share the news about Jesus. The disciples were always on the go. They actively did what God called them to do.

1. Locate the references from the book of Acts, and draw a matching line to the correct descriptions of what the disciples used the Holy Spirit's power to do.

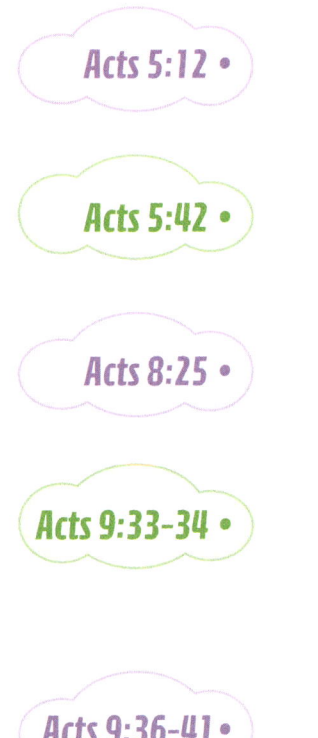

- Acts 5:12 •
- Acts 5:42 •
- Acts 8:25 •
- Acts 9:33-34 •
- Acts 9:36-41 •

- preach in Samaritan villages
- raise a woman from the dead
- heal a man in the name of Jesus
- preach about Jesus in the temple and in houses
- do signs and wonders

2. What are some things you have seen Christians do through God's power?

_____

_____

_____

_____

_____

Name _____

Equipping the Disciples 5.3

The Bible gives examples of how God works to **transform** lives. Write the name of each person God transformed.

1. His job made Jewish people angry
Because he took their money.
Then Jesus said, "Follow me,"
And he became one of the first disciples.

_____ (Matthew 9:9)

2. He doubted Jesus
And would not believe.
Jesus showed His scars.
Now seeing them, he was changed.

_____ (John 20:24–29)

3. List two words in each arrow to describe your life before and after Jesus transformed you. If you have not asked Jesus to be your Savior and you would like to do so, let your teacher know.

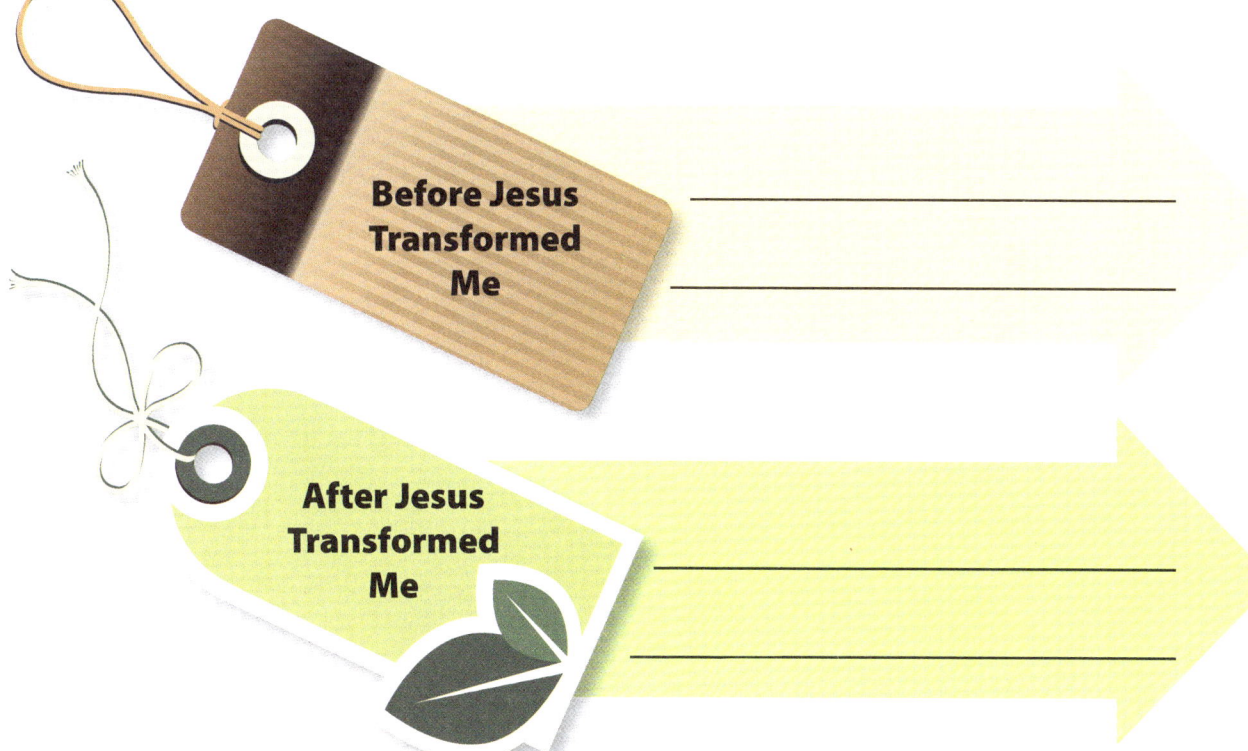

Before Jesus Transformed Me
_____
_____

After Jesus Transformed Me
_____
_____

5.4 Equipping the Disciples

1. You can grow in Christ in many ways. Color each Bible verse leaf the same color as the sentence that describes the verse.

Get involved in serving others.
Rely on prayer.
Obey the Holy Spirit.
Wisely read God's Word.

2. Check each box, and write on each line to show ways you will commit to God. He will continue to help you change and grow.

 I will serve others. One way I will do this is …

_____.

 I will pray regularly. A good time to do this is …

_____.

 I will listen to the Holy Spirit when He wants me to change. An area in which I need to change is …

_____.

 I will read God's Word regularly. A good time to do this is …

_____.

Name _____

The Beatitudes 6.1

Both Matthew and Luke wrote down Jesus' teaching about being **blessed**. Compare Matthew 5:3–6 and Luke 6:20–21. Fill in the blank with the word or words Luke used to describe each **beatitude**.

1. **Matthew 5:3** poor in spirit
   reward: kingdom of heaven

   Luke 6:20 _____
   reward: _____
   _____

2. **Matthew 5:6** hunger and thirst for (after) righteousness
   reward: be filled or satisfied

   Luke 6:21a _____
   reward: _____
   _____

3. **Matthew 5:4** mourn
   reward: comforted

   Luke 6:21b _____
   reward: _____
   _____

4. Write about a time when you felt blessed by God, not by things.

_____
_____
_____
_____

6.2 The Beatitudes

Use Matthew 5:3–10 to help guide you through the maze.

Name _____

The Beatitudes 6.3

1. Write a sentence to explain which beatitude this boy might be showing.

   _____

   _____

   _____

2. Write a sentence to explain which beatitude is needed in this situation.

   _____

   _____

   _____

   _____

3. Write a sentence to explain how you could show the beatitude of being meek at school.

   _____

   _____

   _____

6.4 The Beatitudes

Describe how you can be salt in each of these places.

1. in a store: _____

_____

_____

_____

2. at the playground: _____

_____

_____

3. in your neighborhood: _____

_____

_____

4. Draw a picture of one way you can allow God's light to shine through you today.

Name _____

Building on the Rock 7.3

Building your life on God's Word gives you wisdom. Read the Scripture inside each paint swatch. Circle the phrase that best completes the sentence.

1. When my mom tells me to clean my room, I should …

be sure to do it later.

immediately obey without complaining.

2. When a friend wants to know about Jesus, I should …

wait to learn everything about God's Word before saying anything.

refer to God's Word and tell what God has done for me.

3. When I am unsure about God's plan for me, I should …

ask God to direct me as I make my plans.

do what I think is best.

4. Color the boxes that show wise choices for your life.

7.4 Building on the Rock

Bible truth: 1 Corinthians 3:11

1. Pray. Ask God for wisdom.

2. Think. Ask yourself what the passage of Scripture is saying. Write a question that relates to the meaning.

_____

_____

3. Apply. Write a real-life story that applies the meaning of the passage to your life.

_____

_____

_____

_____

_____

4. Act. Write a question for others to think about that will help them understand the Bible truth and act on it.

_____

_____

Name _____

"I Am" Statements 8.1

Jesus used "I am" statements to teach **truth** about Himself. These helped the Jewish people remember the way God helped them in the past. Look up the Scriptures, and finish the sentences.

1. Exodus 16:31—God sent _____.

This met the Israelites' need to _____
_____.

2. John 6:35—"I am" the _____
_____.

This meets my need for _____
_____.

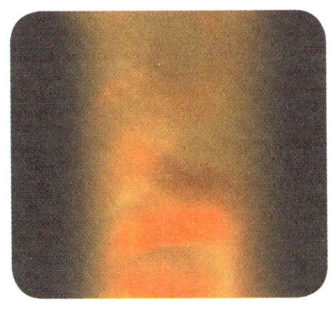

3. Exodus 13:21—God sent a _____
of fire.

This met the Israelites' need to _____
_____.

4. John 9:5—"I am" the _____
_____.

This meets my need for _____
_____.

8.2 "I Am" Statements

1. Genesis 4:2
2. Genesis 21:27
3. 1 Samuel 16:19
4. Exodus 3:1

Look up the verses. Write the shepherd's name you see in the verse.

1. _____
2. _____
3. _____
4. _____

Unscramble the letters to tell something the Good Shepherd does for His sheep.

5. _____ for them
   s r a e c

6. _____ them
   s t r o p e c t

7. _____ with them
   t s y a s

8. _____ His life for them
   e g v i s

Are you one of Jesus' sheep?

Name _____

"I Am" Statements 8.3

Read each situation. Write the need each person has. Find the letter of the "I am" statement that will meet the need, and then write the letter. You may use more than one letter for each "I am" statement.

"I am"	a. Bread of Life	c. Light of the World	e. Door or Gate
	b. way, truth, and life	d. resurrection and life	f. Good Shepherd

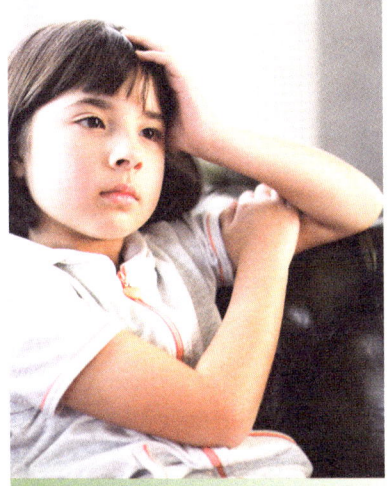

1. Ling wonders if anyone cares about her. Her parents are not home much, and she does not have many friends.

Need: _____

_____

"I am" statement: _____

2. Marco's friend says there are many ways to get to heaven. Marco wonders whether to believe his friend.

Need: _____

_____

"I am" statement: _____

3. Juan feels confused. He does not know the truth about God. He is hungry to know God and wants someone to guide him to God.

Need: _____

_____

"I am" statement: _____

Bible Grade 3

8.4 "I Am" Statements

Jesus described His relationship with His followers as a vine and its branches. Use the lines on the vine to write Jesus' instructions in John 15.

1. verse 2
2. verse 4
3. verse 10
4. verse 12

5. Choose one of the instructions. Write about how you can put it into practice.

_____
_____
_____

Name _____

The Lord's Prayer 9.1

Prayer is talking with God. Complete the following sentences about prayer:

1. I usually pray when _____
_____
_____.

2. Prayer is like talking to a friend because
_____
_____.

3. I should come to God in **submission**
because _____
_____.

4. The place at home I like to pray is
_____
_____.

5. I want to talk to God _____
_____
_____.

Bible Grade 3

9.2 The Lord's Prayer

1. Read the Lord's Prayer in Matthew 6:9–13. Put the following parts of the Lord's Prayer in order:

 Your name is holy, and we honor and praise You.

 Give us all we need today.

 Dear heavenly Father,

 Protect us from anything that might cause us to sin and from evil and Satan.

 Forgive us for our sins, just as we will forgive others.

 Reign as the King on the earth, and do Your will here as You do in heaven.

2. Color every space that contains an **l** or a **p** to find the hidden word.

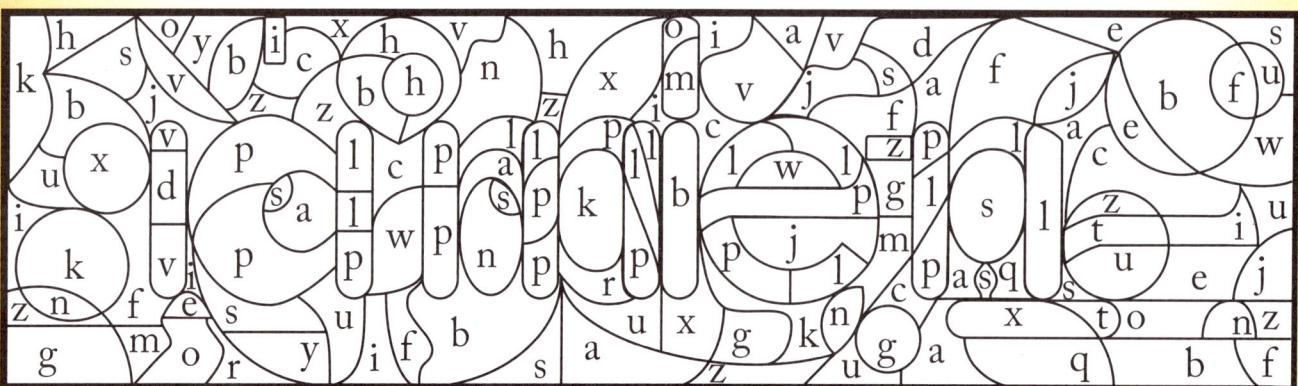

34

Name _____

Walking in Love  10.1

Read each situation. Use the Word Bank to choose a word that shows what your **motive** might be.

WORD BANK

| jealousy | pride | love for God | kindness | selfishness |

1. You and your family serve meals at the homeless shelter.

   _____

2. You do not share one of your bottles of water with your thirsty friend on the way home from baseball practice.

   _____

3. At lunchtime, you sit next to the new classmate.

   _____

4. You loudly announce that you have received an A on your math test.

   _____

5. You hide your sister's ribbon that she won in the art contest.

   _____

6. Write a sentence to tell what you can do at school today to show God's love.

   _____

10.2 Walking in Love

For Exercises 1–3, look up the verses, and answer the questions.

1. Matthew 8:5–10 and 8:13

Jesus showed love to a _____.

For Jewish people, he was difficult to love because he was a Roman, the enemy of the Jewish people.

Jesus showed love by _____ his servant.

2. Mark 1:40–42

Jesus showed love to a man with _____.

For Jewish people, he was difficult to love because healthy people were not supposed to be anywhere near people with this disease.

Jesus showed love by _____ him.

3. Luke 19:2–5

Jesus showed love to _____.

For Jewish people, he was difficult to love because the Jewish people thought tax collectors were thieves.

Jesus showed love by _____ to his house.

4. Think of someone who is difficult for you to love. Then finish this sentence:

I can show love to this person by _____

_____.

Walking in Love 10.3

1. Decode the message that defines selfless.

Code Box

| 1 = a | 2 = c | 3 = e | 4 = f | 5 = g | 6 = h | 7 = i |
| 8 = l | 9 = n | 10 = o | 11 = r | 12 = s | 13 = t | 14 = v |

having concern
6 1 14 7 9 5   2 10 9 2 3 11 9

for others, not
4 10 11   10 13 6 3 11 12   9 10 13

for oneself
4 10 11   10 9 3 12 3 8 4

2. Write God's command found in John 15:17. _____

3. Draw a picture of yourself showing selfless love or concern to someone.

10.4 Walking in Love

1. Read 1 Corinthians 13:4–8. Write the letter for each answer from the Word List by recording it in the correct category.

Love Always …	Word List	Love Never …
_____	a. suffers long (is patient)	_____
_____	b. is kind	_____
_____	c. envies	_____
_____	d. parades itself (boasts)	_____
_____	e. is puffed up (proud)	_____
_____	f. behaves rudely (is rude)	_____
_____	g. seeks its own (is self-seeking)	_____
	h. is provoked (angered)	_____
	i. thinks evil (keeps record of wrongs)	_____
	j. rejoices in iniquity (delights in evil)	_____
	k. rejoices in truth	
	l. bears all things (protects)	
	m. believes all things (trusts)	
	n. hopes all things	
	o. endures all things (perseveres)	
	p. fails	

2. Choose any answer from the Love Always column, and write how you will apply the answer so that you walk in love.

_____

_____

Name _____

Born Again 11.1

1. Jesus used four comparisons when He spoke with Nicodemus (John 3:1–21). Read each verse. Write the correct letter of the comparison above the verse.

a. living by the truth

c. the Holy Spirit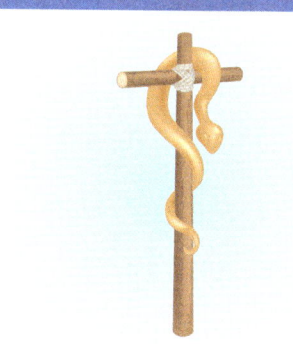

b. born again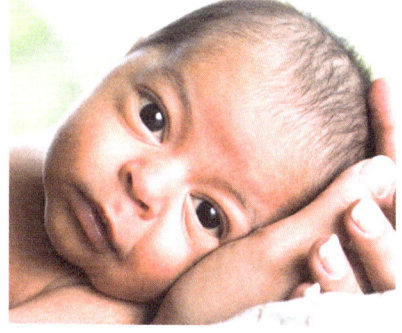

d. Jesus lifted up

____ verse 3

____ verse 8

____ verse 14

____ verses 19–21

2. Finish the definition of <mark>born again</mark>: having accepted _____ as _____.

11.2 Born Again

These Bible verses show the road to salvation and eternal life. Read each verse, and fill in the blank. Stamp each verse according to your teacher's instruction.

1. Romans 3:10 No one is _____.

UNDERSTAND? ☐   AGREE? ☐   WANT TO KNOW MORE? ☐

2. Roman 3:23 Everyone has _____ and fallen short of God's glory.

UNDERSTAND? ☐   AGREE? ☐   WANT TO KNOW MORE? ☐

3. Romans 6:23 The payment for sin is _____, but God's free gift is eternal life through Jesus Christ.

UNDERSTAND? ☐   AGREE? ☐   WANT TO KNOW MORE? ☐

4. Romans 5:8 God loves you. He sent _____ because you have sinned.

UNDERSTAND? ☐   AGREE? ☐   WANT TO KNOW MORE? ☐

5. Roman 10:9 If you say that Jesus is _____ and believe this in your heart, then you are saved.

UNDERSTAND? ☐   AGREE? ☐   WANT TO KNOW MORE? ☐

6. Romans 10:13 _____ calls on the name of Jesus will be saved.

UNDERSTAND? ☐   AGREE? ☐   WANT TO KNOW MORE? ☐

Name _____

Born Again  11.3

1. The Bible uses several word pictures to describe salvation. Read the verses, and draw a line to match each verse with the picture that represents it.

| John 3:3 | Colossians 1:13 | Ephesians 2:19 |

2. Read 1 Corinthians 6:11. Draw what you think happens in this verse.

11.4 Born Again

Read Colossians 3:8–10 and 3:12–17.

1. Write four qualities of the old man, or self.

a. _____

b. _____

c. _____

d. _____

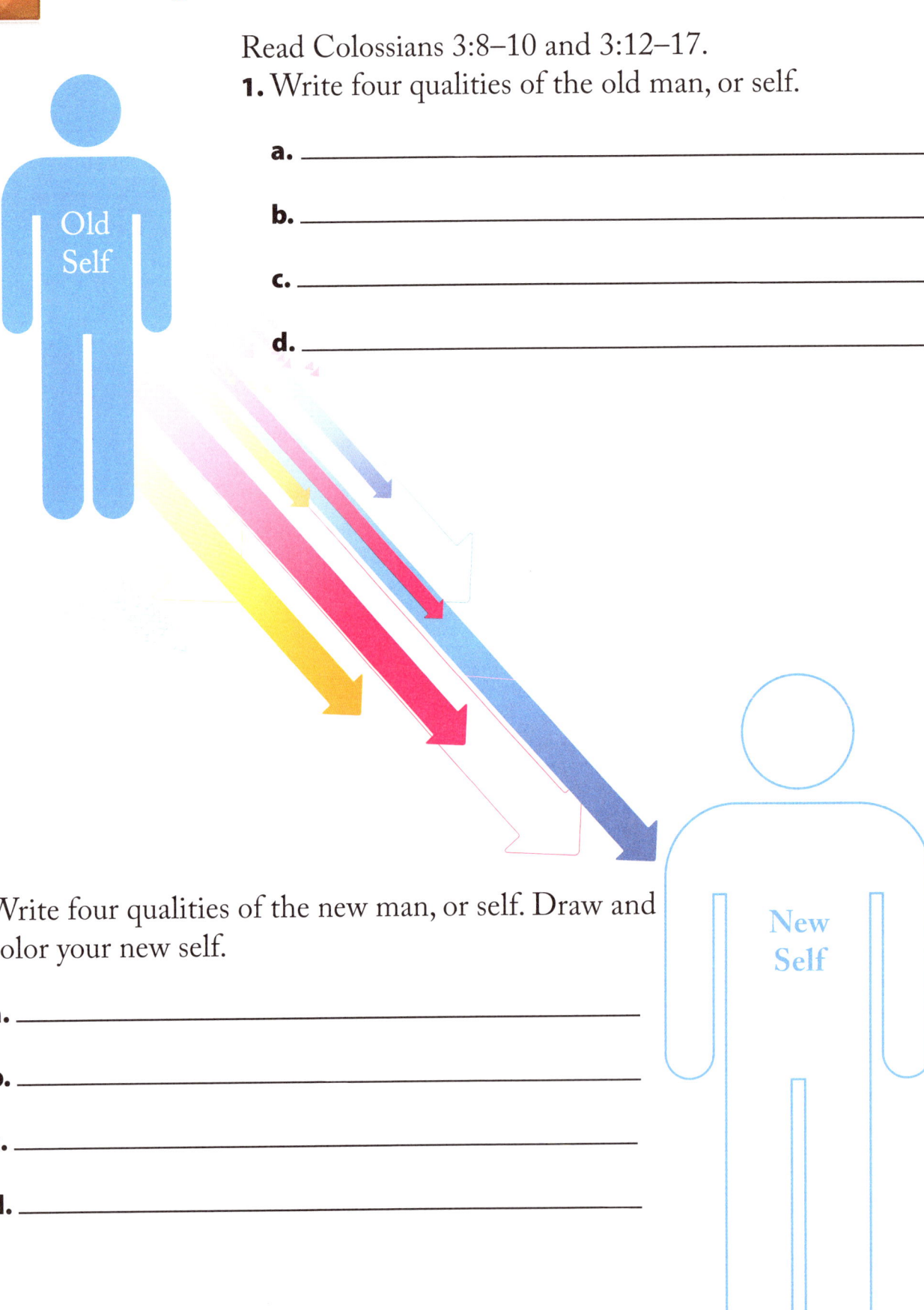

2. Write four qualities of the new man, or self. Draw and color your new self.

a. _____

b. _____

c. _____

d. _____

Name _____

Responding to the Gospel 12.1

1. Draw each stage in the life cycle of a plant.

seed → sprout → seedling → young plant → mature plant →

2. Read the story. Underline the things that help a seed grow. Circle the things that prevent a seed from growing into a mature plant.

Timmy wanted to know how best to make seeds grow. He went to talk to Farmer Zeke to find out. Farmer Zeke explained to Timmy that all farmers should sow their seeds in good soil. Seeds need to be watered regularly. They need sunlight. Farmer Zeke said that seeds will not sprout and seedlings can die if the soil is not in good condition.

Timmy wanted to know if that was all. Farmer Zeke just laughed and smiled. He said that farmers must have much patience as they wait for the time to reap. Seeds do not grow overnight!

3. Why is it important to understand the parable of the sower?

_____

_____

12.2 Responding to the Gospel

1. Look up Luke 8:4–8 and 8:11–15 to read about the person who went out to sow seed. Write the letter of the description that goes with each picture.

____   ____   ____   ____

a. people who hear the Word of God but do not believe it because it is snatched away

b. people who respond to hearing the Word of God but fall away when temptation or testing comes

c. people who accept the Word of God but do not grow because of cares or worries, riches, and pleasures

d. people who accept the Word of God, grow, and share it with others

2. Why is it important to sow God's Word?

_____
_____
_____
_____
_____
_____
_____

Name _____

Responding to the Gospel 12.3

Read the journal entries from missionaries who have shared the ==gospel== with others. Write the letter of the type of soil described by the journal entries.

| a. wayside or path | b. rock | c. thorns | d. good ground or soil |

☐ **1.** Phnom Pen, Cambodia
July 8

Today I told Hanong about Jesus. I invited her to come to a meeting to hear more about Jesus. She told me she is going to another meeting instead. I think the meeting she is going to is to worship the spirits of her ancestors.

☐ **2.** Munich, Germany
May 22

I am so excited! Anja came to class today and told me that both of her parents accepted Jesus. Now they want to come to Bible study too!

☐ **3.** Otavalo, Ecuador
January 10

I asked José why he stopped going to church. He used to be so eager. He says he would still like to hear more about God, but his friends have made fun of him for believing in Jesus.

4. Write about a situation in which you heard God's Word and how you responded. What type of soil were you?

_____

12.4 Responding to the Gospel

As believers spend time on their relationship with God, their faith becomes stronger. When God's Word is sown in people who are ready to accept Jesus Christ as Savior, their faith begins to grow.

1. Circle how Christians can grow in their faith and enjoy God.

praying • worshipping God • having fellowship with other believers • choosing to tell the truth • reading the Bible • listening to God • treating others well • obeying God • serving others

2. When you share your faith with others, you are sowing a seed into the soil of their heart. You are also growing in your own faith. Write the names of three people you want to tell about Jesus. Plan how and when you will tell them about Jesus.

a. _____

b. _____

c. _____

Name _____

Thanksgiving 13.1

WORD BANK

scribe	thankfulness	Samaritan's	deafness	priest
cleansed	two	Jew's	mercy	nine
faith	dancing	inside	one	pity

Look up Luke 17:11–19. Ten men suffered from leprosy. Write the words from the Word Bank to complete the sentences. You will not use all the words in the Word Bank.

1. A _____ decided if a person had leprosy.

2. The men asked Jesus to have _____ on them.

3. As the men went to see the priests, they were _____.

4. After Jesus healed the men, _____ came back to give glory and praise to God and to thank Jesus.

5. Jesus commented about the _____ faith.

6. Describe why all the men should have been thankful.

_____

_____

_____

© Bible Grade 3

13.2 Thanksgiving

Read the verses to complete the sentences and answer the questions.

1. Read Psalm 92:1. It is good to thank and praise God because …

   _____
   _____
   _____.

2. Read Psalm 92:2. What qualities does this psalm say to praise God for?

   _____
   _____

3. According to Psalm 92:4, I can be thankful because of _____
   _____.

4. Read Psalm 147:8–9. What three things God made can you be thankful for?

   a. _____
   b. _____
   c. _____

5. Read Psalm 100:4. God wants people to enter His gates with
   _____ and His
   courts with _____.

6. Write the name of a song you sing that gives thanks and praise to God. How does the song help you thank and praise Him?

   _____
   _____

Name _____

Thanksgiving 13.3

Write what the student in each hard situation might say as a thanks to God.

1.

_____
_____
_____
_____

2.

_____
_____
_____
_____

3.

_____
_____
_____
_____

13.4 Thanksgiving

Write words or phrases about being thankful to finish the acrostic.

T _____
H _____
A _____
N _____
K _____
S _____

Seeking the Lost 14.1

Good news

Complete the phrases to explain the gospel.

Who is Jesus?

1. the Son of _____ (John 1:34)

2. the _____, the _____, the _____ (John 14:6)

What has Jesus done for people?

3. has come to save _____ (1 Timothy 1:15)

4. _____ for sins, was _____, and _____ the third day (1 Corinthians 15:3–4)

Why should someone say yes to the gospel?

5. to have _____ life (John 5:24)

6. to become _____ of God (John 1:12)

7. to accept the _____ of God (Ephesians 2:8–9)

8. Write the definition of evangelism.

_____

_____

14.2 Seeking the Lost

1. Look up Romans 5:8, and write what God showed and what Jesus Christ did.

God showed _____ to people when Christ _____ for sinners.

2. Jesus cares about lost people and wants you to also. Read the real-life devotion by eight-year-old Abbigayle. She cared and shared the gospel.

My new friend

Have you ever done something that God said to do that was hard? I have. God told me to go visit an elderly lady, so I did. The lady was so blessed that she cried tears of happiness! I gave her a Bible, and she read it over and over. I think she came to know God, and I am so happy for her! The best thing is she will be with Jesus forever!

Even though it was uncomfortable at first, I'm thankful I gave up my time to go see her and share God's message.

3. You can show you care about lost people by sharing the gospel with them. Write what you will tell someone about Jesus.

_____

_____

_____

_____

Name _____

Seeking the Lost 14.3

Write the letter of the parable by each description of something from the parable. There can be more than one answer for each item.

a. the lost sheep   **b.** the lost coin   **c.** the lost son

1. Someone searches for something lost. _____

2. Someone repents. _____

3. Someone rejoices or celebrates. _____

4. Someone shows compassion. _____

5. Someone wants to reconcile. _____

6. Choose one of the three parables. Draw a picture showing the rejoicing when the lost became found.

14.4 Seeking the Lost

Draw a line along the path by choosing facts about David Livingstone. You will take him to the village of people who have never heard about Jesus.

Name _____

Forgiving 15.1

When I repent of my sins,
God is faithful to forgive me.

Look up the words in the Glossary, and write the definition for each.

1. Repent: _____
_____
_____

2. Forgiveness: _____
_____

Sin is anything you think, feel, say, or do that does not meet God's perfect standard. On the lines, write two common sins. In the box, draw a picture of yourself turning your back to those sins and focusing on God.

3. Sins that offend God:

a. _____
_____
_____

b. _____
_____
_____

15.2 Forgiving

Answer the questions.

In the parable about forgiveness, how do you think it felt …

1. for the servant to go before the king to ask for forgiveness?

_____

2. for the servant to have his debt forgiven or canceled?

_____

Forgiveness removes the distance in a relationship that sin causes. Psalm 103:12 reveals that God removes sins as far as the east is from the west.

Look up Psalm 103:12, and write how this verse applies to your life.

3. _____

_____

_____

Name _____

Forgiving 15.3

Help these friends "bridge" their hurts. On each bridge below, write a godly solution that includes forgiveness.

1. Alicia loaned Melanie her math book. Melanie returned it with its cover torn off. When Alicia asked her what happened, Melanie said she did not know. What could Alicia do to keep her friendship with Melanie and keep her things in good condition?

   _____

   _____

2. Tom forgot to invite Sam to his birthday party. Now Sam is upset. What could Tom do to make it up to Sam?

   _____

   _____

3. When Mrs. Nyberg asked who took a key off her desk, Roberto lied and said Victor did. Victor was upset about the lie. What could Victor do to be able to trust Roberto again?

   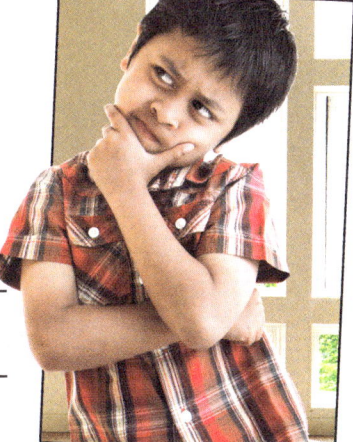

   _____

   _____

Bible Grade 3

15.4 Forgiving

It is important to repent and ask for forgiveness when you have done something wrong. It is also important to forgive when someone has hurt you.

1. Write a story about someone who needed to ask for forgiveness and someone who needed to forgive.

_____
_____
_____
_____
_____
_____
_____
_____
_____
_____
_____
_____
_____

2. What life lesson did your characters learn about forgiveness?

_____
_____
_____

Name _____

Stewardship 16.1

Color the coins that show the true statements from Matthew 25:14–30.

1. The master, or lord, trusted three servants with money.

2. All the servants hid their money.

3. The third servant was allowed to keep his talent.

4. The master praised both of the servants who showed good stewardship.

5. The master rewarded one faithful servant with another talent.

6. Draw a picture of what you would do to be a good steward if you received money. Label your drawing.

16.2 Stewardship

Read this devotion by nine-year-old Emily:

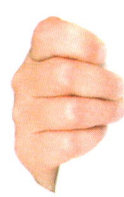

Are you talented? I remember a time when I had a talent and I used it for God. I had an ability of cup stacking. Cup stacking is a sport where you stack cups in a pattern and win medals if you do it really fast. I went to a cup-stacking competition. There was a lot of pressure on me. On the second day of the competition, I did my cup stacking and won a medal for tenth in the world! I prayed that others would see God's power, love, and light shine in me as I did cup stacking.

Matthew 25:14-30 says that God trusts each person with a special talent. It may be money, time, or something special, like cup stacking. I learned it is important to use these talents for Him.

1. How are you using an ability you have to bring honor to God?

_____

_____

_____

Circle **F** and then every other letter. Write the circled letters on the line below to complete the sentence.

2. I can be _____ in using my talents for God.

Name _____

Stewardship 16.3

Read the Bible verses. Circle the word **good** or **poor** for the kind of choice the people made about stewardship. Write a sentence about how each person made a good or poor choice.

1.

   the widow
   Mark 12:43–44

   good   poor

   _____
   _____
   _____

3.

   the rich young man
   Matthew 19:21–22

   good   poor

   _____
   _____
   _____

2.

   the church
   2 Corinthians 8:3

   good   poor

   _____
   _____
   _____

4. Read 1 Peter 4:10. Write this verse about stewardship in your own words.

   _____
   _____
   _____
   _____
   _____
   _____
   _____
   _____

16.4 Stewardship

Complete the sentences.

Possessions

1. I have extra _____ I could give to someone.

2. I could use my _____ to help someone learn about God.

3. I can show God's love to someone by sharing my _____ _____.

Abilities

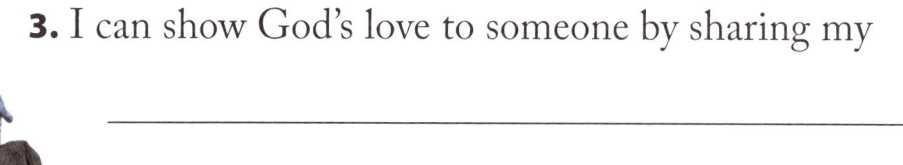

4. I am good at _____. I can be a faithful steward of this ability by _____ _____.

5. I like to _____. I can use this to help people know about God by _____ _____.

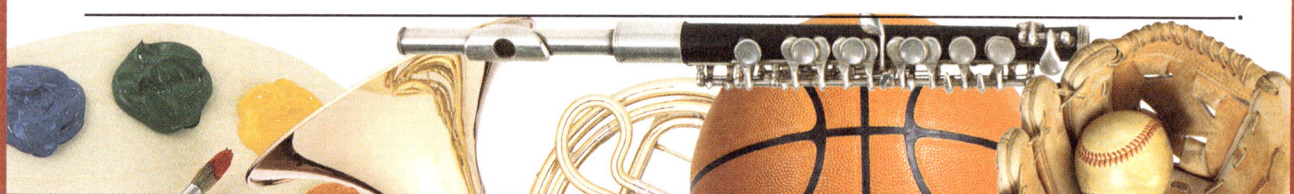

Time

6. I have time before _____ to read the Bible.

7. I have time after _____ to tell someone about Jesus.

Name _____

Christmas 17.1

God used prophets to tell people about Jesus' birth. Look up the New Testament verses. Draw a line to match each Old Testament prophecy about Jesus to the Scripture passages in the New Testament that show it has been fulfilled.

Old Testament Prophecy   **New Testament Fulfillment**

1. Family Line (Jesse) •   • Matthew 1:18–23,
   (Isaiah 11:1–2)   Luke 1:26–35

2. Throne of David •   • Matthew 1:1,
   (Isaiah 9:7)   Luke 1:32

3. Others Honor Jesus •   • Matthew 2:1–6,
   (Psalm 72:10–11)   Luke 2:4, John 7:42

4. The Mother of Jesus •   • Matthew 1:6,
   (Isaiah 7:13–14)   Acts 13:22–23

5. Birthplace •   • Matthew 2:1–2 and 2:7–11
   (Micah 5:2)

6. One of the prophecies stated that others would show honor to Jesus. In what ways can you show honor to Jesus?

   _____

   _____

   _____

   _____

   _____

17.2 Christmas

1. Circle three facts about baby Jesus. Underline three mistakes.

He is God's Son.

He was born in Bethel.

He is from the line of Nebuchadnezzar.

When He came, He was not a king.

He is perfect.

He is divine.

Now write new sentences to correct the mistakes.

2. _____

3. _____

4. _____

5. What is another fact you know about Jesus? _____
_____

6. Name a prophecy that Jesus fulfilled by coming to the earth.
_____
_____

Christmas 17.3

1. Complete the code, which explains why God is omnipotent.

Code Box

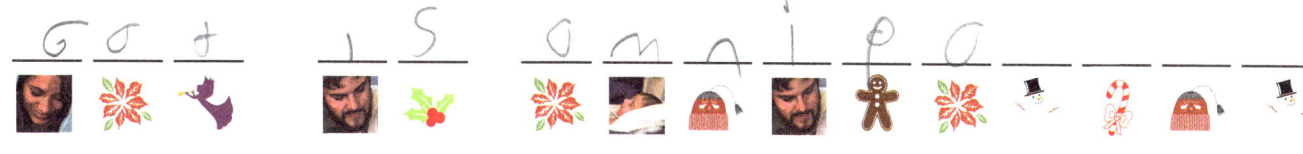

G o d _ _ i s _ o m n i p o _ _ _ _ _

_ _ _ _ _ _ _ _ _ _ _ _ _ _ _

_ _ _ _ _ _ _!

Make sentences by completing the following:

2. Gabriel's announcement of Jesus' birth was special because _____.

3. God has shown His omnipotence by _____.

4. I have seen God's power when _____.

17.4 Christmas

1. Describe two ways the wise men honored Jesus.

a. _____

_____

b. _____

_____

2. Finish the phrases to make complete sentences about honoring and worshipping God.

I can honor God by _____.

I can worship God with _____.

I want to honor God for _____.

I worship God because _____.

I can worship God after _____.

I will honor God because _____.

I can worship God among _____.

I can honor God during _____.

Name _____

Jesus' First Miracle 18.1

The Bible records <mark>miracle</mark>s of God. God's miracles show His omnipotence. They help people believe in God.

Read the first Bible verse below. Then make a check mark (✓) in each column where the heading is true for that verse. Leave the column blank if the verse does not match the heading. Do the same for the other verses.

Bible verse	This records a miracle of God.	This shows God's omnipotence.	This records more belief in God because of one of His miracles.
1. Genesis 11:9			
2. Exodus 14:19–22 and 14:31			
3. Ruth 4:8			
4. Joshua 1:15			
5. Daniel 6:21–23 and 6:25–26			

6. The verses you just read are from the Old Testament. The New Testament records miracles too. What would a miracle Jesus did in the New Testament tell you about Him?

   _____

7. How would you recognize a miracle of God if it happened in your life or the life of someone you know?

   _____

   _____

Bible Grade 3

18.2 Jesus' First Miracle

Refer to John 2:1–11. Circle the wrong word in each sentence below. Then, write the correct word on the line.

1. One day Jesus, Jesus' mother, and Jesus' friends went to a wedding in Jerusalem, a village. _____

2. The feast continued so long that the guests ran out of water. _____

3. Jesus' friends asked Jesus to help. _____

4. Jesus told the servants to fill the waterpots with tea. _____

5. The servants disobeyed. _____

6. Then Jesus told the servants to take a drink to the master of the village. _____

7. The master wondered why the feast ended with such bad wine. _____

8. The servants knew they had poured water into the waterpots, but now it was juice. _____

9. Peter had performed a miracle! _____

Name _____

Jesus' First Miracle 18.3

Hebrews 11 lists many people who had great faith in God. Unscramble the names of these people listed in the Bible's Hall of Faith.

1. _____
   LEAB (verse 4)

2. _____
   OCHNE (verse 5)

3. _____
   AHON (verse 7)

4. _____
   MABAARH (verse 8)

5. _____
   HRASA (verse 11)

6. _____
   ACSIA (verse 20)

7. _____
   CABOJ (verse 21)

8. _____
   SHEJOP (verse 22)

9. _____
   OMESS (verse 23)

Would you like to be in the Hall of Faith? Write about how you showed faith in God for something.

10. By faith _____ your name _____ _____.

11. Tell some of the ways God provided for the people above through His omnipotence.

_____
_____

Bible Grade 3   71

18.4 Jesus' First Miracle

1. Write the words from the Word Bank to complete the ==testimony== about God's omnipotence.

WORD BANK
- prayed
- George Mueller
- ship
- faith
- miracle
- captain

Miracle of the Disappearing Fog

_____ was a man of faith in God. He was on a _____ headed to Canada to speak at a meeting. He talked to the ship's _____ about a problem. The bad weather meant the ship would not arrive in time for the meeting. George _____. Suddenly the fog was gone! The captain knew that God's omnipotence had caused a _____. The captain shared his testimony of God's provision with others to help them have _____ in God.

2. Draw a picture of the event.

Name _____

Jesus Satisfies 19.1

Jesus multiplied the loaves and fish to feed the crowd of people. Multiply the numbers below to discover a special message. Find the answer to each problem, and then use the code to write the correct letter in each shaded box. The first one is done for you.

Code Box

1. $\begin{array}{r}3\\\times 3\\\hline 9\end{array}$ $\begin{array}{r}1\\\times 1\\\hline\end{array}$ $\begin{array}{r}8\\\times 1\\\hline\end{array}$ $\begin{array}{r}3\\\times 2\\\hline\end{array}$ $\begin{array}{r}2\\\times 4\\\hline\end{array}$

1 – e   5 – l   8 – s   11 – f
2 – m   6 – u   9 – J   12 – d
3 – n   7 – a   10 – y   13 – t
4 – i

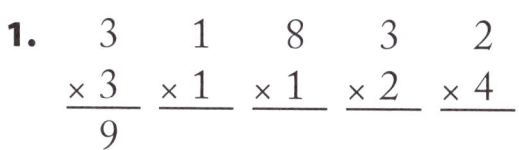

J ▮ ▮ ▮ ▮

$\begin{array}{r}4\\\times 2\\\hline\end{array}$ $\begin{array}{r}7\\\times 1\\\hline\end{array}$ $\begin{array}{r}13\\\times 1\\\hline\end{array}$ $\begin{array}{r}2\\\times 2\\\hline\end{array}$ $\begin{array}{r}4\\\times 2\\\hline\end{array}$ $\begin{array}{r}11\\\times 1\\\hline\end{array}$ $\begin{array}{r}4\\\times 1\\\hline\end{array}$ $\begin{array}{r}1\\\times 1\\\hline\end{array}$ $\begin{array}{r}1\\\times 8\\\hline\end{array}$

▮ ▮ ▮ ▮ ▮ ▮ ▮ ▮ ▮

$\begin{array}{r}7\\\times 1\\\hline\end{array}$ $\begin{array}{r}1\\\times 5\\\hline\end{array}$ $\begin{array}{r}5\\\times 1\\\hline\end{array}$ $\begin{array}{r}2\\\times 1\\\hline\end{array}$ $\begin{array}{r}5\\\times 2\\\hline\end{array}$ $\begin{array}{r}3\\\times 1\\\hline\end{array}$ $\begin{array}{r}1\\\times 1\\\hline\end{array}$ $\begin{array}{r}1\\\times 1\\\hline\end{array}$ $\begin{array}{r}4\\\times 3\\\hline\end{array}$ $\begin{array}{r}2\\\times 4\\\hline\end{array}$

▮ ▮ ▮ ▮ ▮ ▮ ▮ ▮ ▮ ▮

How do you think …

2. the disciples felt about trying to feed so many people?

_____

3. Jesus felt about the crowd, knowing they were hungry? _____

_____

4. the people felt waiting to be fed? _____

5. Write the definition of <mark>compassion</mark>. _____

_____

Bible Grade 3   73

19.2 Jesus Satisfies

1. Read each sentence. Circle the loaf if that detail appeared in Matthew's Gospel. Circle the fish if that detail appeared in John's Gospel. Circle both pictures if the detail appeared in both accounts.

	Matthew (14:13-21)	John (6:1-14)
a. Then Jesus told the disciples to feed the crowd.	🍞	🐟
b. Jesus tested Philip.	🍞	🐟
c. Jesus asked for the loaves and fish.	🍞	🐟
d. Andrew brought forward a boy who had loaves and fish in his lunch.	🍞	🐟
e. Jesus told the crowd to be seated.	🍞	🐟
f. Jesus blessed, or gave thanks for, the food.	🍞	🐟
g. Jesus gave the food to the disciples to pass out to the crowd.	🍞	🐟
h. The disciples collected 12 baskets of leftover loaves and fish.	🍞	🐟

2. Pretend you are the boy with the five loaves and two fish. Write about how it felt to hand your food to someone else, and then watch Jesus feed 5,000 people with your lunch! Use words from Exercise 1.

_____

_____

_____

_____

_____

Name _____

Jesus Satisfies 19.3

1. Number the events listed below in the correct order.

_____ The unclean, evil spirits begged for permission to enter the pigs.

_____ Jesus told the man to return home to tell others what He had done for him.

_____ The man from Gadera had unclean, evil spirits. He went to meet Jesus.

_____ Jesus commanded the unclean, evil spirits to leave the man.

_____ The pigs ran off the cliff.

2. Jesus proved He has authority over unclean, evil spirits. Write a cadence of praise about Jesus' power. Make lines one and two rhyme with each other. Do the same with lines three and four.

SOUND OFF! 1, 2!
SOUND OFF! 3, 4!
1, 2, 3, 4, 1, 2—3, 4!

_____
_____
_____
_____
_____

3. What need can Jesus' power and authority satisfy in your life?

_____
_____

19.4 Jesus Satisfies

Satan tries to weaken believers' faith by telling lies. Believers should use God's Word in spiritual warfare to defend themselves. Read the lies on the left. Then draw a line to match each arrow with the verse of truth written on the shield.

1. Being a Christian means that you are not going to have any friends.

2. You lied to your teacher. God will never forgive you.

3. You did not know what to say when the kid across the street asked you why you go to a Christian school. You must not really be a good witness for Christ.

4. Your dad was just laid off from work again and your mom is in the hospital. God must not care for you.

5. You cannot draw or memorize Bible verses as well as others. You are not valuable.

 Psalm 34:15

 Psalm 139:14

 Proverbs 18:24

 Psalm 103:10–12

 Acts 1:8

Name _____

Walking on Water 20.1

God's power over nature appears throughout the Bible. Look up these Scriptures and fill in the blanks.

1. Job 9:8 God treads (walks) on the _____.

2. Psalm 65:7 God stilled _____.

3. Isaiah 43:16 God made a _____.

4. Find the letters that match the color of the blank. Choose the correct letter to complete the message.

When Jesus walked on water, He showed

_m _i _o _ _n _e.

20.2 Walking on Water

When things distract you, get your **focus** back on Jesus. Write the first letter and then write every other letter in the row of letters. Discover some ways to focus on Jesus to keep a strong relationship with God!

r m e t a i d a y p o s u w r e B n i o b d l y e

1. ___ ___ ___ ___   ___ ___ ___ ___   ___ ___ ___ ___

p o r t a l y

2. ___ ___ ___ ___

w k o v r u s c h f i o p

3. ___ ___ ___ ___ ___ ___ ___

m y e r m j o n r x i e z h e j v i e d r l s m e z s

4. ___ ___ ___ ___ ___ ___ ___   ___ ___ ___ ___ ___

5. Peter trusted Jesus and walked on the water to Him. Show that you can trust Jesus and draw yourself walking on the water to Jesus.

Name _____

Walking on Water 20.3

1. Read this true devotion written by nine-year-old Sophia.

Have you ever felt very scared? One day on my birthday my mom came home and told me she had cancer! I was really scared. All these questions kept running through my mind like a lightning storm! Can she die? Is she going to be sick for years? I was so scared. Then I read Psalm 56:4. God calmed my heart and helped me to trust in Him. My mom came through the cancer treatment and is doing great now. I thank God for helping me through that hard time and helping me not to be afraid. We can trust God always to be with us through hard times.

2. Describe how Jesus is **trustworthy** in your life.

_____

_____

_____

3. Write a thank-you message to God for bringing you through a fearful, stormy time.

20.4 Walking on Water

Follow the clues to change each word. Jesus is the remedy to change any fear to faith in Him.

1. fear - e = _____

2. far - r + ir = _____

3. fair - r + th = _____

4. Choose five colors. Match the reference with its remedy to fear by coloring them the same color.

- Philippians 4:19
- Psalm 68:35
- God helps you.
- God supplies for your needs.
- God gives understanding.
- 1 John 5:20
- God gives power.
- 1 Peter 5:7
- Isaiah 41:10
- God cares.

80

Healing a Blind Man — 21.1

1. Number the first set of events from John 9:1–7 in the order they happened.

_____ The disciples asked Jesus if the blind man or his parents had sinned.

_____ Jesus saw a man born blind.

_____ Jesus told the disciples that the man's blindness was not because the man or his parents had sinned.

_____ The disciples believed the man was blind as a result of sin.

2. Number the last set of events from John 9:1–7 in the order they happened.

_____ The blind man was healed and began to see.

_____ Jesus told the blind man to go wash in the pool of Siloam.

_____ Jesus spat on the ground, made clay or mud, and put it on the man's eyes.

_____ Jesus explained that God's work should be displayed through the blind man.

3. The blind man could see for the first time in his life. What do you think he wanted to see first? _____

21.2 Healing a Blind Man

Read the following sentences about John 9:8–34. Make an **X** in the box under the correct heading for each sentence.

	shows spiritual blindness	shows spiritual sight
1. "Say that God healed you and not Jesus!"	☐	☐
2. "The man who healed you is a sinner!"	☐	☐
3. "I do know that I once was blind and now I can see."	☐	☐
4. "I am telling you the truth about this man, but you are not listening to me."	☐	☐
5. "We do not know anything about this man!"	☐	☐
6. "God hears those who worship Him and follow in His will."	☐	☐
7. "How could this man heal me if He were not from God?"	☐	☐
8. "You are a sinner and you are trying to lecture or teach us!"	☐	☐

Unscramble the words to complete the sentence.

9. The _____ had spiritual blindness because

    H I S E P R A E S

they did not see the _____ about Jesus. They did not have

    H R T T U

_____ in Him.

    T H A I F

82

Name_____

Healing a Blind Man  21.3

1. Circle the words that describe spiritual sight and how the healed man demonstrated spiritual sight.

God's desire for relationship

courageous

sleepy

not interested

speaking boldly

faith

unbelief

light of the world

responding

Match the four truths of spiritual sight on the left side to their meanings on the right side.

2. God's desire for relationship •   • Jesus wants to have a relationship with everyone.

3. Faith •   • reacting or answering

4. Responding •   • Jesus shows God's work.

5. Light of the world •   • a strong belief or trust in something

6. How do people show they have spiritual sight? Write your answers on the glasses.

They have faith in_____.   They respond by_____.

21.4 Healing a Blind Man

Use the code below to decode the missing words in the paragraph.

1 = y	6 = s	11 = m	16 = g
2 = w	7 = r	12 = l	17 = e
3 = v	8 = p	13 = k	18 = d
4 = u	9 = o	14 = i	19 = c
5 = t	10 = n	15 = h	20 = b
			21 = a

The Ability to See

When Jesus saw the ___ ___ ___ ___ ___ man, He knew that the blind
    20 12 14 10 18

man needed both ___ ___ ___ ___ ___ ___ ___ ___ sight and
                 8 15 1   6 14 19 21 12

___ ___ ___ ___ ___ ___ ___ ___ sight. Jesus saw
 6   8 14   7 14   5   4 21 12

___ ___ ___ ___ ___ ___ ___ as an act of ___ ___ ___ ___ rather than
15 17 21 12 14 10 16   12   9   3 17

___ ___ ___ ___, as the ___ ___ ___ ___ ___ ___ ___ ___ ___ thought.
 2   9   7 13   8 15 21   7 14   6 17 17   6

You can see Jesus' omnipotence, ___ ___ ___ ___ ___ ___ ___ ___, mercy,
                                 18 14   3 14 10 14   5   1

and ___ ___ ___ ___ ___ ___ ___ ___ ___ ___
    19   9 11   8 21   6   6 14   9 10

throughout His ___ ___ ___ ___ ___ ___ ___ ___.
               11 14 10 14   6   5   7   1

Name _____

Lazarus Lives 22.1

Jesus chose to do things that would <mark>glorify</mark> God. Look up each Scripture and write ways you could bring praise and honor to God.

1. I can glorify or honor God in my
   _____.
   (1 Corinthians 6:20)

2. I can glorify God when I _____ or

    _____ or whatever I _____.
   (1 Corinthians 10:31)

3. I can glorify God in _____.
   (1 Peter 4:11)

4. Draw a picture of how you could glorify God.

22.2 Lazarus Lives

Look up the Scriptures and complete the first two statements. Complete the rest of the statements with your own thoughts.

1. If you mourn, you will be

   _____.

   (Matthew 5:4)

2. If someone believes in Jesus and dies, then

   _____.

   (John 11:25)

3. If I believe Jesus died for my sins, then

   _____
   _____
   _____.

4. If I pray, then _____
   _____
   _____.

5. If I trust in God's power, then

   _____
   _____
   _____.

Name _____

Lazarus Lives 22.3

Lazarus had his grave clothes removed and put on clothes for living. Believers in Jesus should choose new behaviors to replace their sinful habits.

Read Colossians 3:12 and 3:14. On the numbered clothes, write the new clothing that shows someone is spiritually alive.

22.4 Lazarus Lives

Miracles

The following sentences are about Jesus' miracles. Fill in the missing words.

1. Jesus turned water into _____ at a wedding in **Cana**.

2. **Jesus** _____ over 5,000 people.

3. Jesus cast out the evil _____ and cast them into **pigs**.

4. Jesus and **Peter** walked on _____.

5. Jesus **healed** a _____ man.

6. Jesus raised **Lazarus** from the _____.

7. Find and circle the six words from the lines and the six **bold** words. The words can be across or down.

```
Y  L  B  F  E  D  Z  B  H  V
S  A  L  D  U  W  A  T  E  R
R  Z  I  E  P  I  G  S  A  J
C  A  N  A  E  N  J  Q  L  E
B  R  D  D  T  E  G  Z  E  S
K  U  Y  A  E  H  L  K  D  U
T  S  P  I  R  I  T  S  G  S
```

88

© Bible Grade 3

Name _____

The Transfiguration 23.1

Read each sentence and circle either **T** if it is true or **F** if it is false.

1. Peter said that Jesus was the Christ of God. **T F**

2. Jesus asked the disciples to tell others that He was the Christ. **T F**

3. To deny yourself means to give up everything you need to do. **T F**

4. You are to take up your cross only in difficult times. **T F**

5. To follow Jesus means to live like God wants you to. **T F**

6. Those who follow Jesus will always have an easy life. **T F**

7. When you take up your cross, you put God's will first. **T F**

Jesus told His followers to be willing to take up their cross and follow Him. You might suffer because you choose to follow Jesus. Read each situation and write how you could respond to the suffering in a way that pleases God.

8. If my friend does not invite me to his party because I am a Christian, I can _____.

9. If my neighbor laughs at me when I go to church, I can _____.

23.2 The Transfiguration

1. Read the account of the **transfiguration** of Jesus in Matthew 17:1–9. Draw the missing pictures. Then number the pictures in order of events and list the verse or verses that each picture represents.

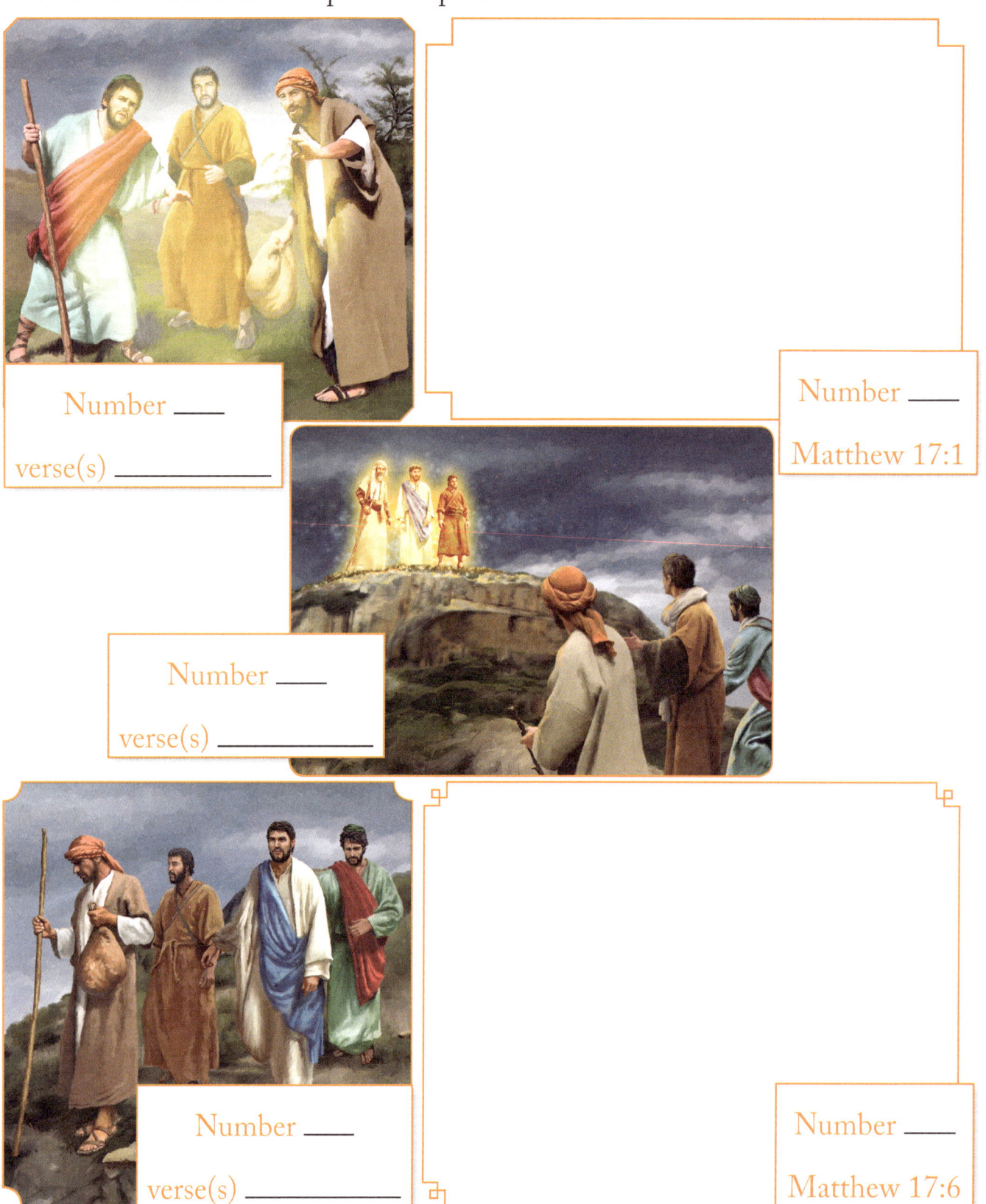

Number ____

verse(s) _____

Number ____

Matthew 17:1

Number ____

verse(s) _____

Number ____

verse(s) _____

Number ____

Matthew 17:6

90

Name _____

The Transfiguration 23.3

1. Read the Scripture verses. Fill in the chart with the missing information about each **mediator**.

Name	Moses	Elijah	Jesus
Role in God's plan			
Scripture	John 1:17	Deuteronomy 18:18	1 John 4:14

2. Help Ramiro discover some of the ways God shows how to be involved in God's plan. Trace the correct path of ways that God speaks to people.

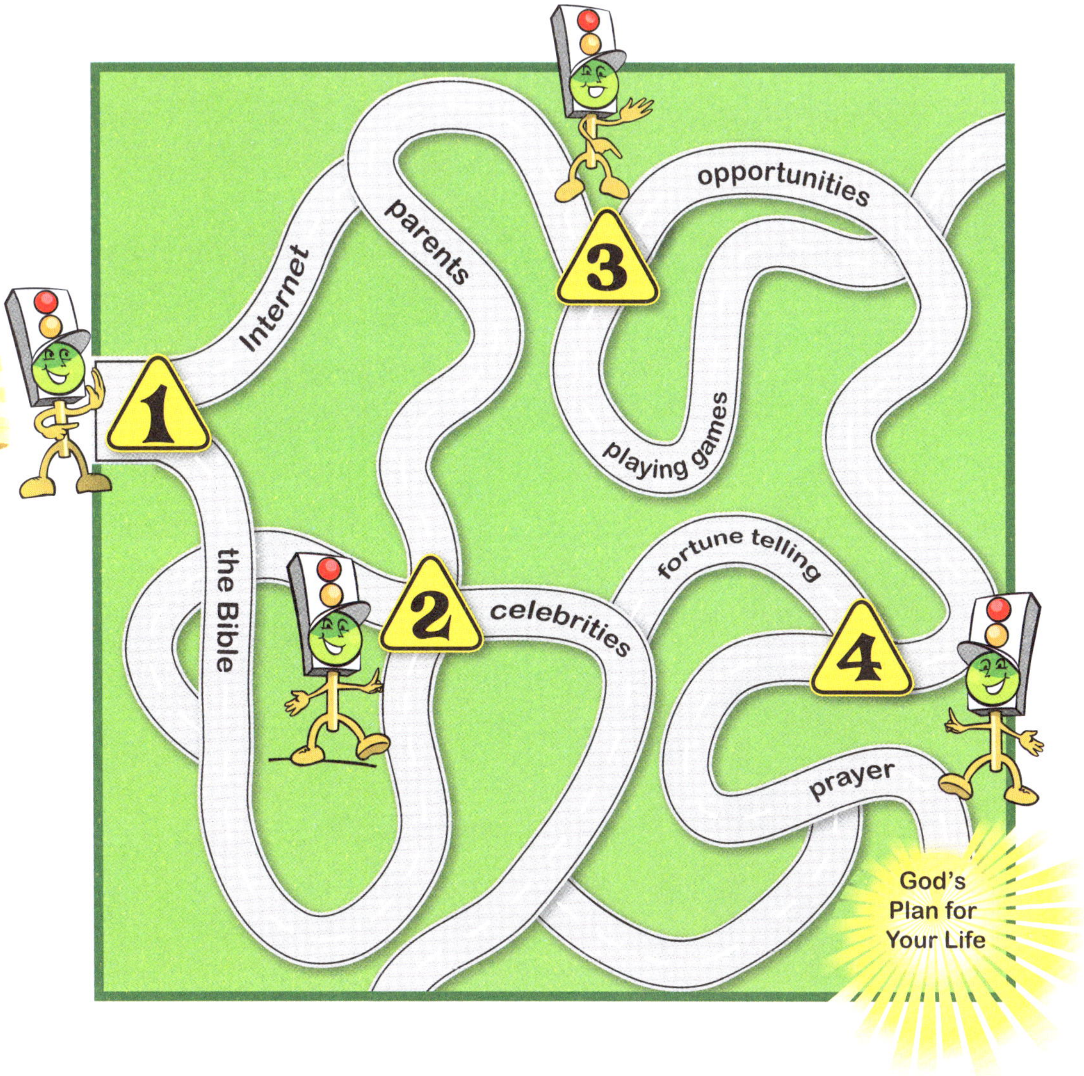

23.4 The Transfiguration

Read each story. Look up the Scripture verses and fill in the circle that helps each person understand how to follow God's plan for his or her life.

1. Stephan's parents have decided to be missionaries to the Chinese people. The family now has to sell their house and raise money for the move to China. "None of my friends has to do this!" Stephan whines. He does not think that China is a good plan for his family.

    ○ Psalm 60:1
    ○ 2 Corinthians 5:21
    ○ Jeremiah 29:11

2. Ian wants to go to summer camp, but his neighbor asked Ian to help their family provide a neighborhood Bible camp. He really wants to have fun with his friends at the summer camp, but he knows the neighbor kids need to hear about Jesus. Ian wonders what he should do.

    ○ Acts 17:24
    ○ Proverbs 3:5
    ○ Romans 6:23

3. Izza's friends want her to join them in teasing the new girl in their neighborhood. They think the girl looks and acts differently from them. The new girl seems lonely and keeps watching them ride their bikes. Izza wants her friends to like her.

    ○ Romans 12:2
    ○ Numbers 14:1
    ○ Ephesians 6:1

Name _____

The Holy Spirit 24.1

Circle the correct answer to each question about Pentecost.

1. Where did Jewish people go to celebrate Pentecost?

   a. Bethlehem   **b.** Cana   **c.** Jerusalem

2. What had God promised to the believers?

   a. the Holy Spirit   **b.** an easy life   **c.** no more sin

3. What sound did the people hear?

   a. thunder   **b.** drums   **c.** wind

4. Where did the believers see something like flames?

   a. above their heads   **b.** beside the candles   **c.** on the wall

5. What did the Jewish visitors to the city hear?

   a. their own language   **b.** bells ringing   **c.** singing

6. Write two to three sentences thanking God for sending the Holy Spirit to be with all believers.

   _____

   _____

24.2 The Holy Spirit

Read Acts 2:38–39.

1. What gift does God give believers in Him?

_____

_____

2. This gift was for the believers listening to Peter, to these believers' children, and all who _____. That means you!

3. Peter talked to thousands of people gathered during Pentecost. Name four places where you could witness to someone.

_____   _____

_____   _____

4. Color every space in the box that contains an **h** or an **s** to find the word to complete the sentence.

The Holy Spirit helps believers to _____.

94

Name _____

The Holy Spirit 24.3

According to Acts 1:15 and 2:1–3, the Holy Spirit gave power to the disciples and other believers gathered in Jerusalem. Read the Bible verses, and complete the sentences to show the difference the Holy Spirit made in Jesus' followers.

1. Instead of being **afraid**, (Luke 8:24–25)  they spoke the word of God _____ _____. (Acts 4:31)

2. Instead of being **selfish**, (Luke 9:46)  they _____ _____ _____. (Acts 4:32)

3. Instead of **leaving** Jesus alone, (John 16:32) 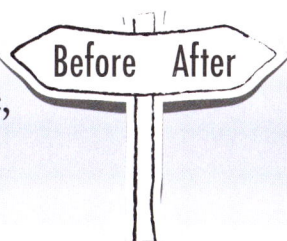 they _____ _____ teaching and preaching about Jesus. (Acts 5:42)

4. Draw a picture below of something the new believers did that showed the Holy Spirit was helping them be like Jesus. (Acts 2:42–47)

24.4 The Holy Spirit

The Holy Spirit will help you witness. On the line by each situation, write the Scripture that shows a solution to the problem.

WORD BANK

| 2 Timothy 2:24 | Romans 1:16 | 2 Peter 1:20–21 |

1. Some of my friends are not believers. I feel uneasy about witnessing because they might laugh at me.

_____

2. My cousin said the Bible is full of made-up stories. I am not sure what to say to him.

_____

3. My friend argues that her religion is right and that Jesus is not God's Son.

_____

4. Jesus wants His followers to tell others about Him. Write a prayer asking the Holy Spirit to help you share God's Word with others.

Dear God,

_____
_____
_____
_____
_____

Name _____

Peter Is Transformed 25.1

1. Look up restore in the Glossary and write the definition.

_____

_____

2. Read 1 John 1:9. Then read this true-life devotion by Chase.

> Have you ever been tempted to steal? Well I have and it's not pleasant. My cousins and I went to a bowling alley. We had fun bowling and then went over to the gaming area to play some games. When we ran out of money, my cousin showed me how the machine was broken so you could get free games. I was impressed that he knew that. Then I tried to do it. It was fun, so I kept going. I even got many free tickets from the machine to redeem prizes. My cousin did it, I did it, and my friend did it. It was like stealing from the machine! Soon we got caught. I felt really bad. I mean really bad. I gave the tickets back and told the manager I was sorry. I'm glad God forgave me. Since then I have learned to be a person that is honest and encourages others to do what is right for God.

3. Write a sentence about how Chase's relationship with God was restored.

_____

_____

25.2 Peter Is Transformed

God's forgiveness restored Peter, and Peter acted with ==boldness==. Read Mark 11:25. God's forgiveness reminds people to restore relationships. For each question, read the three good choices. Circle one you would choose to do.

1. A friend hears you sharing the gospel and walks away. What will you do?

    a. Look for a time to say something nice.

    b. Pray for my friend.

    c. Ask God to help me forgive hurt feelings.

2. Your best friend chooses to play a game with other students rather than go on the swings with you. What will you do?

    a. Cheer for my friend.

    b. Ask if I can play the game too.

    c. Invite my friend to swing another time.

3. Some of your friends have a party, but they do not invite you. What will you do?

    a. Plan a party and invite them.

    b. Tell them I am happy they had so much fun.

    c. Ask if they want to do homework together.

4. Complete each sentence.

    I feel sorry when _____.

    I feel restored when _____.

    I can forgive others when _____.

    I see change in my life when _____.

Name _____

Peter Is Transformed 25.3

1. Read the following true story. Underline words that show how Jonathan followed Jesus.

> Spreading the gospel was important to Jonathan's parents. They took the family on a trip to another country. They played with children at an orphanage and made friends with the people there. Jonathan had fun, but he did not always want to do what he was supposed to do. Sometimes he caused trouble. His parents talked with him, and Jonathan felt sorry for causing problems. He knew that if he repented God would forgive him, so he asked God for forgiveness.
>
> The family went on more trips to other countries. Jonathan handed out Bibles, but he did not feel ready to talk boldly about God's Word. He prayed that God would help him share the good news about Jesus. On one trip, Jonathan became friends with Rafael. Jonathan shared his faith and prayed with his new friend to receive Christ.

2. What can you learn from Jonathan about following Jesus?

_____

_____

3. Write some advice you would give a friend who has decided to follow Jesus more closely.

_____

_____

25.4 Peter Is Transformed

Read the Bible verse at each stop on the Road to Restoration. In the sign, write one word you think is most important to you.

Name _____

Stephen and the Early Church 26.1

Read the Scriptures and write who selflessly served others. Draw a line to match the person with the way the person served.

1. Acts 9:39 _____ •   • helped Paul and others

2. Luke 10:33–34 _____ •   • washed others' feet

3. John 13:3–5 _____ •   • helped an injured person

4. Romans 16:1–2 _____ •   • sewed clothing

5. Why did their relationship with God motivate these people to serve?

_____

_____

6. Explain one way you will serve someone else today.

_____

_____

_____

26.2 Stephen and the Early Church

1. Stephen was the first <mark>martyr</mark> after Jesus' resurrection. Unscramble the letters on the stones to make words. Write each word on the matching colored line to show Stephen's response to people stoning him to death.

Stones: oucsf, ptke, no, ish, uJsse, Speenth

_____ _____ _____ _____
_____ _____ .

Look up the Bible verses and write down how to respond to <mark>persecution</mark>.

2. Matthew 5:44 _____

3. Philippians 4:4 _____

4. Romans 12:14 _____

5. 1 Peter 4:16 _____

Name _____

Stephen and the Early Church 26.3

Fill in the blanks.

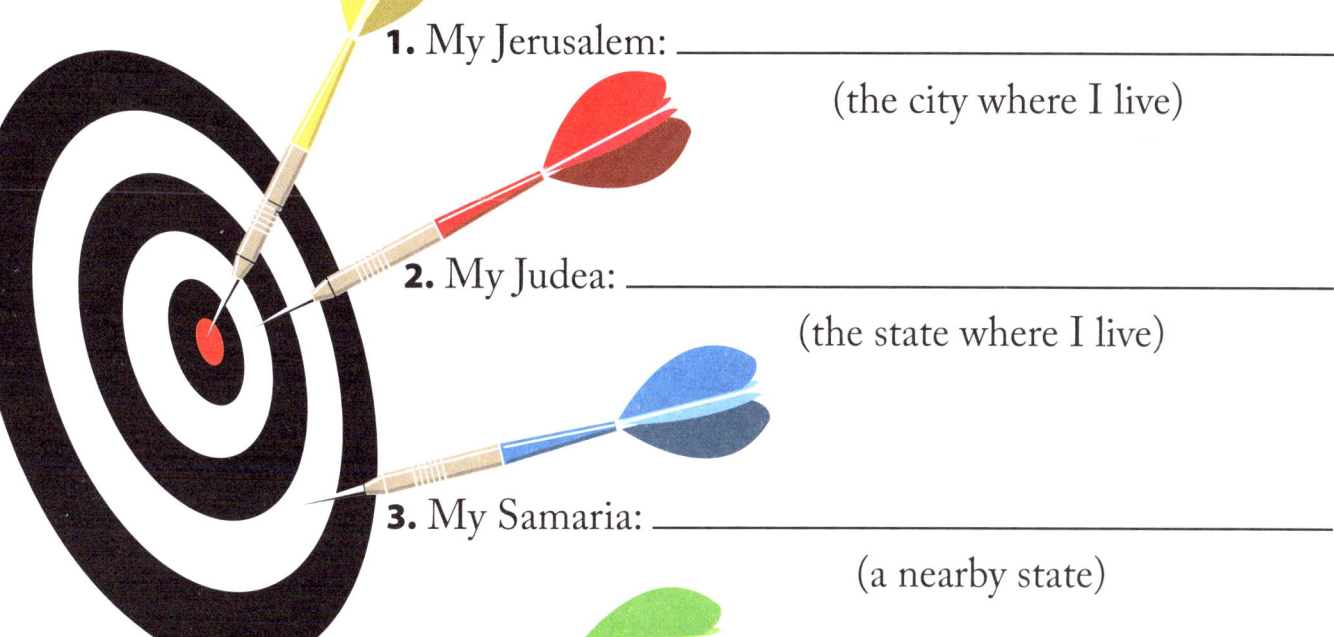

1. My Jerusalem: _____
   (the city where I live)

2. My Judea: _____
   (the state where I live)

3. My Samaria: _____
   (a nearby state)

4. My ends of the earth: _____
   (a place far from where I live)

5. Another people group: _____

6. Draw yourself telling someone in your city about Jesus.

26.4 Stephen and the Early Church

If you suffer for Jesus, your reaction can bring glory to God.
Fill in each blank with a good way to respond to the suffering.

1. If someone teases me for being a Christian, I will _____
_____.

2. If someone does not invite me to a party because I go to church, I will _____
_____.

3. If someone will not play with me because I believe in Jesus, I will _____
_____.

4. If someone laughs at me because I sing praise songs, I will _____
_____.

5. Write a prayer for someone suffering for Jesus.

Dear God,
_____
_____.
   Amen.

Name _____

Saul's Conversion 27.1

1. Circle the correct definition of the word **conversion**.

   a. a silver coin used by the Greeks and worth about a day's wage

   b. the time when a person decides to follow Jesus

   c. one's own desire to take action

Finish each sentence with a word or words from the Word Bank. Copy each letter in a small shaded box into the long box. Keep the letters in order to discover what Jesus gave Saul.

WORD BANK

| God's | on | persecuted | Priest | travel |
| Saul's | High | himself | speak | Jesus |

2. Saul called __ __ __ __ __ __ __ the chief or worst of sinners.

3. Saul did not want the disciples to spread __ __ __ ' __ Word.

4. Saul __ __ __ __ __ __ __ __ __ __ believers in Jesus.

5. Saul asked the __ __ __ __ __ __ __ __ __ __ for permission to __ __ __ __ __ __ to Damascus to find believers.

6. While he was __ __ the road to Damascus, a dazzling light surrounded Saul, and __ __ __ __ __ began to __ __ __ __ __ to him.

7. __ __ __ __ ' __ life was changed that day.

8. _____

© Bible Grade 3   105

27.2 Saul's Conversion

1. Draw Saul on the road with his companions when Jesus spoke to him.

2. Draw Saul praying and waiting for Ananias to come.

3. God gave Saul the free gift of grace and salvation. Write a sentence about yourself and include the words **salvation** and grace.

_____

Name _____

Saul's Conversion 27.3

When Jesus died on the cross, He paid the price for all sin. God's grace is a free gift to all who receive it.

1. On this gift, write at least three wrong things you have done that you know God has forgiven you for.

Circle the answer to complete the sentence. Write it on the line.

2. God's grace shows even greater when people are _____.
 weak   self-confident   strong

3. People _____ whether to accept God's free gift.
 forget   choose   wonder

27.4 Saul's Conversion

1. Believers in Christ are a new creation. Write in each box one thing that has changed in your life because you follow Jesus.

One way I obey God:

One thing I know is true:

One thing I watch or listen to that pleases God:

One way I treat my friends:

2. Read the true-life devotion about God's grace by Justin, age 9.

> Before I knew God, I went to church but I did not really know what it meant. One day in the car on the way to church, I accepted God in my life. After that, I really understood what it meant to trust Jesus. To this day, I am glad that He is my Savior because without Him I would not be able to go to heaven. Romans 6:23 says that God gave me a free gift of eternal life with Jesus. I am also glad that I accepted Jesus because a few months after that my family had some serious problems. I did not go through it alone. God was there to help me along the way. I would feel sad sometimes, but the difference was that I was always comforted when I thought about God taking care of me. He gave me new strength and understanding I did not have before.

God helped Justin. Describe a time when God helped you.

_____

_____

Paul's Early Ministry 28.1

1. Use the code to discover letters of the missing word. Then write those letters in the blanks.

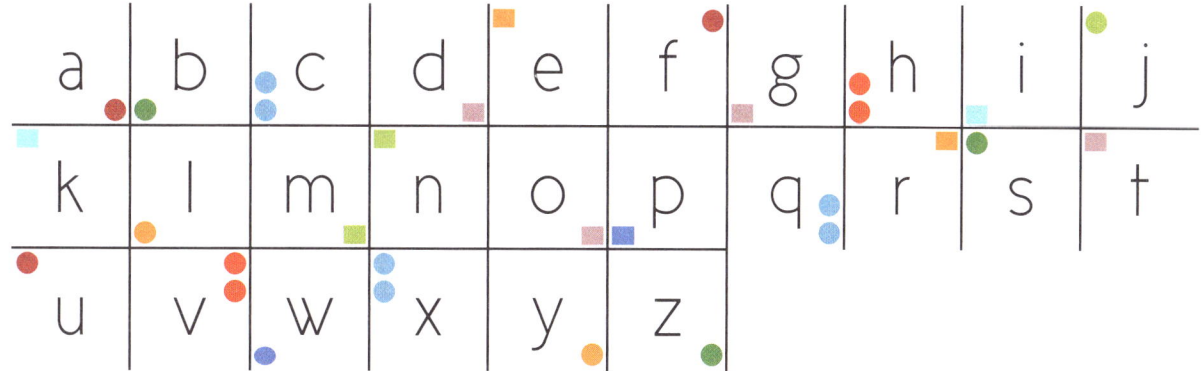

God ___ ___ ___ ___ ___ ___ ___ ___ people to do His work.

People were not sure that Paul had changed. His past actions caused distrust, and his new actions led to trust. Match each of Paul's actions to the word that shows whether the action caused trust or distrust.

2. arrested Christians •

3. believed in Jesus •

4. boldly preached in the synagogue •

5. persecuted believers •

6. stayed with the disciples •

• trust
• distrust

28.2 Paul's Early Ministry

Read Psalm 34:13–14. Fill in the blanks with ways you can prepare now to serve God.

1. Keep your _____ from evil.

2. Keep your _____ from speaking deceit or lies.

3. Depart or turn from _____ and do _____.

4. Seek _____ and _____ it.

Paul studied the Scripture when he was a child. He had a very good education. God called Paul, a Roman citizen, to share the gospel with the Gentiles. Jesus taught Paul even more about Himself. Think about ways God might be preparing you now to serve Him.

5. I like to _____

_____.

6. I am practicing _____

_____.

7. I want to learn _____

_____.

8. How could God use what you enjoy for His glory? _____

_____

_____

Name _____

Paul's Early Ministry 28.3

Circle all the verbs (action words) in the sentences below to review Paul's life after he believed in Jesus.

1. Paul told people about Jesus immediately.

2. Paul preached to the Jewish people in Damascus.

3. Paul spoke boldly about Jesus in Jerusalem.

4. Paul taught the Gentile believers in Antioch.

5. Paul listened to Agabus, the prophet.

6. Along with Barnabas, Paul delivered an offering to believers in Judea.

7. Paul helped others follow God.

Write four verbs from above or think of other verbs that show:

8. Paul was a leader.
   _____
   _____
   _____
   _____

9. Paul worked with others.
   _____
   _____
   _____
   _____

28.4 Paul's Early Ministry

Paul's skills and experiences were stepping-stones along the path of his life to bring glory to God. Think about ways your life can bring glory to God. Write one way you can prepare to serve Him in each of the following areas of life:

1. Family: _____

2. School: _____

3. Friends: _____

4. Church: _____

5. Talents: _____

6. Interests: _____

7. Read 1 Peter 4:10. What is the purpose of using your God-given skills and abilities for Him? _____

Name _____

Easter 29.1

1. Read John 3:16. Write an explanation about what Jesus did to show His great love for you.

_____

_____

2. Look up each Scripture and draw a picture in the space to show what happened based on the verses.

Matthew 26:26–30

John 17:1–5

Matthew 26:14–16

John 12:12–19

3. Write the numbers 1–4 in the circles above to show the correct order of the events.

29.2 Easter

Read each sentence. Circle *selfish* if the sentence is a description of *having more concern for self rather than others*. Circle *selfless* if the sentence is a description about *having more concern for others rather than self*.

1. Soldiers were dividing up Jesus' clothes.

selfish   selfless

2. The soldiers wrote "King of the Jews" on Jesus' cross to mock Him.

selfish   selfless

3. Jesus forgave the people who wanted Him to die.

selfish   selfless

4. Jesus loves you enough to die for you.

selfish   selfless

5. I can pray for those who treat me in an unkind way.

selfish   selfless

6. Draw a line from the cross to the verses describing how God's omnipotent power and love brought salvation to people.

- Philippians 2:5–8
- Matthew 6:1
- 1 Peter 2:24
- Romans 5:6
- Ephesians 6:1

Name _____

Easter 29.3

1. Read Luke 24:1–6. Use the pattern below to write your own poem about when the women discovered the resurrection.

_____
Title (noun)

_____
five-syllable description

_____
seven-syllable description

_____
five-syllable description

2. Look at the shape-person running to the empty tomb. Color the shapes that tell who Jesus showed Himself to after the resurrection.

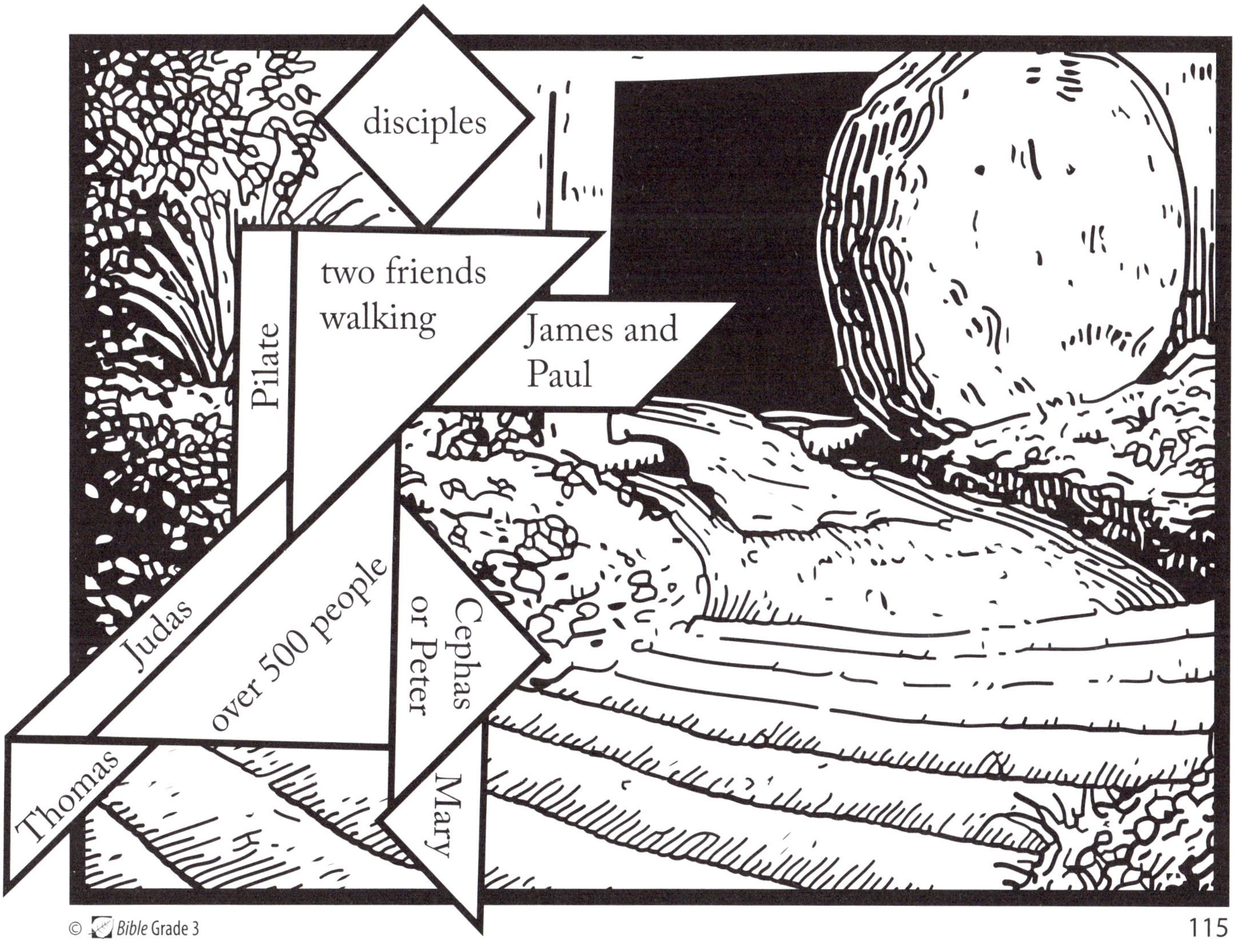

Shapes labeled: disciples, two friends walking, Pilate, James and Paul, Judas, over 500 people, Cephas or Peter, Thomas, Mary

29.4 Easter

Jesus promises eternal life to everyone who believes in Him. Read the verses below. Match each statement on the cross to a verse by coloring the box the same color as the pencil the verse is in.

Name ______________________________

Paul's First Two Missionary Journeys

30.1

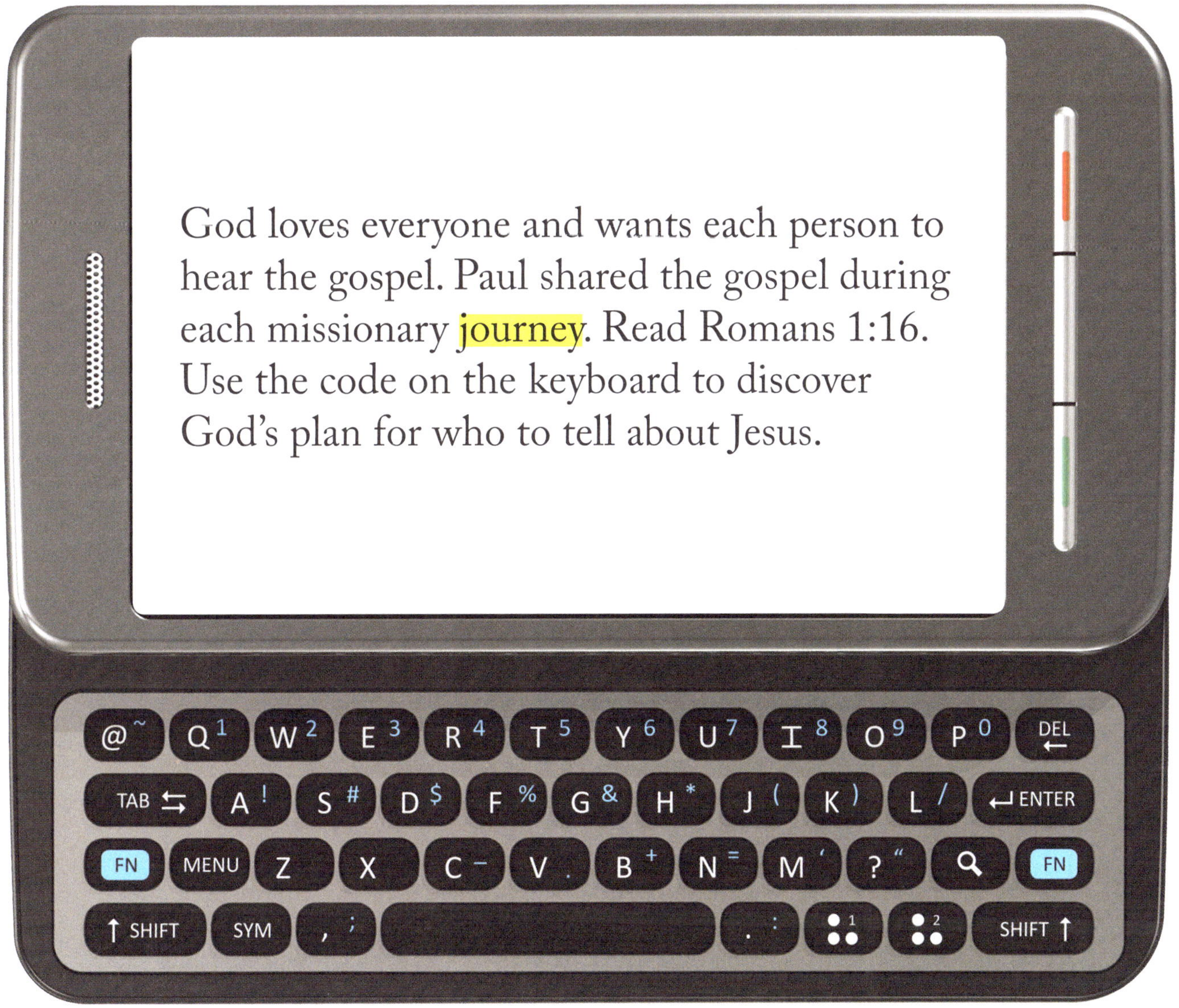

God loves everyone and wants each person to hear the gospel. Paul shared the gospel during each missionary journey. Read Romans 1:16. Use the code on the keyboard to discover God's plan for who to tell about Jesus.

1. God's plan: First, ______ __ ___ ____,

0 4 3 ! – *   5 9   5 * 3   (3 2 #,

then to the ______, __ ________.

& 4 3 3) #,   9 4   & 3 = 5 8 / 3 #.

Read Acts 13:48. How did the Gentiles respond to Paul's bold announcement?

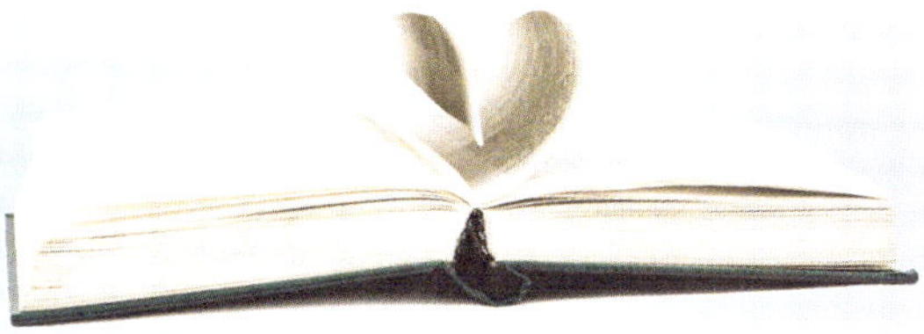

2. They were ______________

and ________________ the word of the Lord.

30.2 Paul's First Two Missionary Journeys

Refer to Acts 16:16–40. Imagine you are a reporter. Read each verse and fill in the details on this article. In the speech bubbles, write words of praise that Paul and Silas might have said while they were in prison in Philippi.

Prison Edition

Philippi Times

50 AD

Slave Girl with an Evil Spirit

Paul

This girl bothered Paul and Silas for many _____. (verse 18) In the name of _____, Paul commanded the spirit to leave. (verse 18) The girl's owners had Paul and Silas beaten and thrown into _____. (verse 23) At _____, Paul and Silas were _____ and _____. (verse 25) After the earthquake, the prison doors _____. (verse 26) The prison keeper asked Paul, "What must I do to be _____?" (verse 30)

PRISON PAINS & PRAYERS

118

Name _____

Paul's First Two Missionary Journeys — 30.3

Even though people persecuted Paul, he chose to **persevere**. In Athens, Paul looked for ways to share the gospel. He saw an altar to an unknown god and told the people about the true God (Acts 17:22–23). Read the verses below and then write an answer that helps tell people about God.

1. Your neighbor comments about the beautiful day. Read Psalm 118:24 and say,

   "_____."

3. At the zoo, someone wonders how the animals came to be unique and amazing. Read Genesis 1:25 and say,

   "_____."

2. Your friend says that no one cares about her. Read 1 Peter 5:7 and tell her,

   "_____."

4. Your aunt comments about how wonderful the food tastes at the restaurant. Read Psalm 34:8 and say,

   "_____."

30.4 Paul's First Two Missionary Journeys

1. Write a thank-you note to Paul for persevering in telling good news about Jesus.

Dear Paul,

_____

_____

Sincerely,

_____

2. Work with a partner and circle words below that relate to Paul's first missionary journey.

3. Now work with your partner and draw a box around the words that relate to Paul's second missionary journey. You may use some words twice.

Barnabas

jail

Priscilla and Aquila

went first to the synagogue

earthquake

hit with stones

preached

persevered

Silas

beaten

worshipped as a god

Timothy

healed a man

Mark

Lydia

Name _____

Paul's Third Journey 31.1

Refer to Acts 19:1–12. Decide if each statement below is true or false. If it is true, put a 😊 in the box. If it is false, put a ☹ in the box. Correct all false statements on the lines provided.

1. Paul's purpose in traveling was to get as much fame as possible.
_____
_____

2. Paul told 12 men that the baptism of John was all they needed.
_____
_____

3. Paul's ministry in Ephesus went on for over two years. He encouraged and equipped the church there. _____
_____

4. Paul chose to endure, and God blessed by doing many miracles through Paul. _____
_____

5. If sick people touched one of Paul's handkerchiefs or aprons, they were healed. _____
_____

6. Very few people in the province of Asia heard God's Word.
_____
_____

31.2 Paul's Third Journey

1. Paul told the truth to people in Ephesus about false gods and the true God. Then a riot broke out. Read the traffic light to discover how the truth can change people. Then look up the Bible verses and fill in the blanks in the sentences based on the Scriptures.

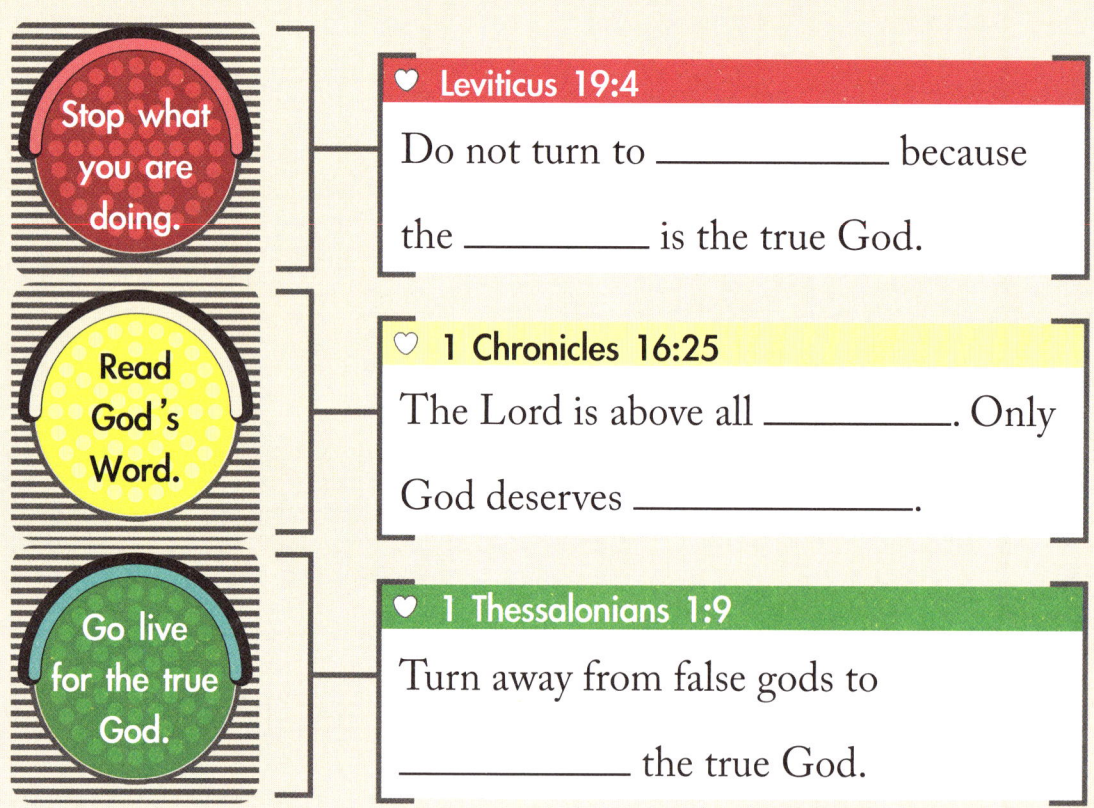

Stop what you are doing.

♥ Leviticus 19:4

Do not turn to _____ because the _____ is the true God.

Read God's Word.

♡ 1 Chronicles 16:25

The Lord is above all _____. Only God deserves _____.

Go live for the true God.

♡ 1 Thessalonians 1:9

Turn away from false gods to _____ the true God.

2. Write a sentence telling how God's Word prepares you to serve Him.

_____

_____

Name _____

Paul's Third Journey 31.3

1. As Paul traveled, he strengthened and encouraged followers of Jesus. Make a check mark next to three ways you can do the same.

- ☐ with a worship song
- ☐ with helpfulness
- ☐ by having God's joy
- ☐ by praying
- ☐ with a psalm
- ☐ with a Bible verse
- ☐ by being faithful
- ☐ by telling Bible truths
- ☐ by sharing with others
- ☐ with God's power

2. Plan some encouraging actions to use the next time these situations happen to you. When you complete the action later, check the "Did It!" box.

The next time …	I will …	Did it!
Mom or Dad needs to relax after a hard day,		☐
my brother, sister, or friend complains about something,		☐
any family member is sad,		☐

31.4 Paul's Third Journey

1. Circle the correct answer for each statement.

When Paul traveled, he _____.

a. complained
b. encouraged others
c. read a good book

When Paul was tired, he _____.

a. gave up
b. took a long rest
c. persevered

When Paul heard bad news, he _____.

a. comforted others
b. changed his plans
c. took a long walk

When Paul's friends asked him not to go to Jerusalem, he _____.

a. changed his plans
b. followed his friends
c. obeyed God

2. Paul urged people to serve God and others. With a partner, read each verse below. Talk about how the verse answers the questions of why, who, and how to serve. Write one key word or phrase from each verse to answer the questions.

Why? (Ephesians 5:1)

_____

Who? (Philippians 2:4)

_____

How? (Colossians 3:23)

_____

Name _____

Paul's Journey to Rome 32.1

Draw a line through the error in each sentence. Based on Acts 27, write the correct word to make a true statement on the blank.

1. Paul was a tourist on a ship. _____

2. The ship was going to Jerusalem. _____

3. There were 20 people on board the ship. _____

4. The passengers on the ship were so worried they could not eat any candy. _____

5. Paul knew they would be safe because he listened to the sailors. _____

6. Some of the people were safely delivered from the shipwreck. _____

Paul chose to be courageous during the ship's long journey. Complete the following sentence.

7. I need God's help to be courageous when _____
_____.

32.2 Paul's Journey to Rome

1. Number the events from Acts 28 in the correct order.

    ____ People on Malta showed hospitality to Paul and all the other passengers.

    ____ Paul healed Publius' father and others through God's power.

    ____ A snake bit Paul's hand.

    ____ God delivered Paul and the others from a shipwreck to the island of Malta.

    ____ The people on the island were amazed that Paul did not die.

2. Write a prayer you think Paul might have prayed on the island of Malta.

    Dear God,

    _____

    _____

    _____

    _____

    _____

    _____

    Amen

Name _____

Paul's Journey to Rome   32.3

Paul wrote several books in the Bible to believers in many towns. Follow the arrows from each book to find the name of the place where the believers lived. Write the town's name on the line.

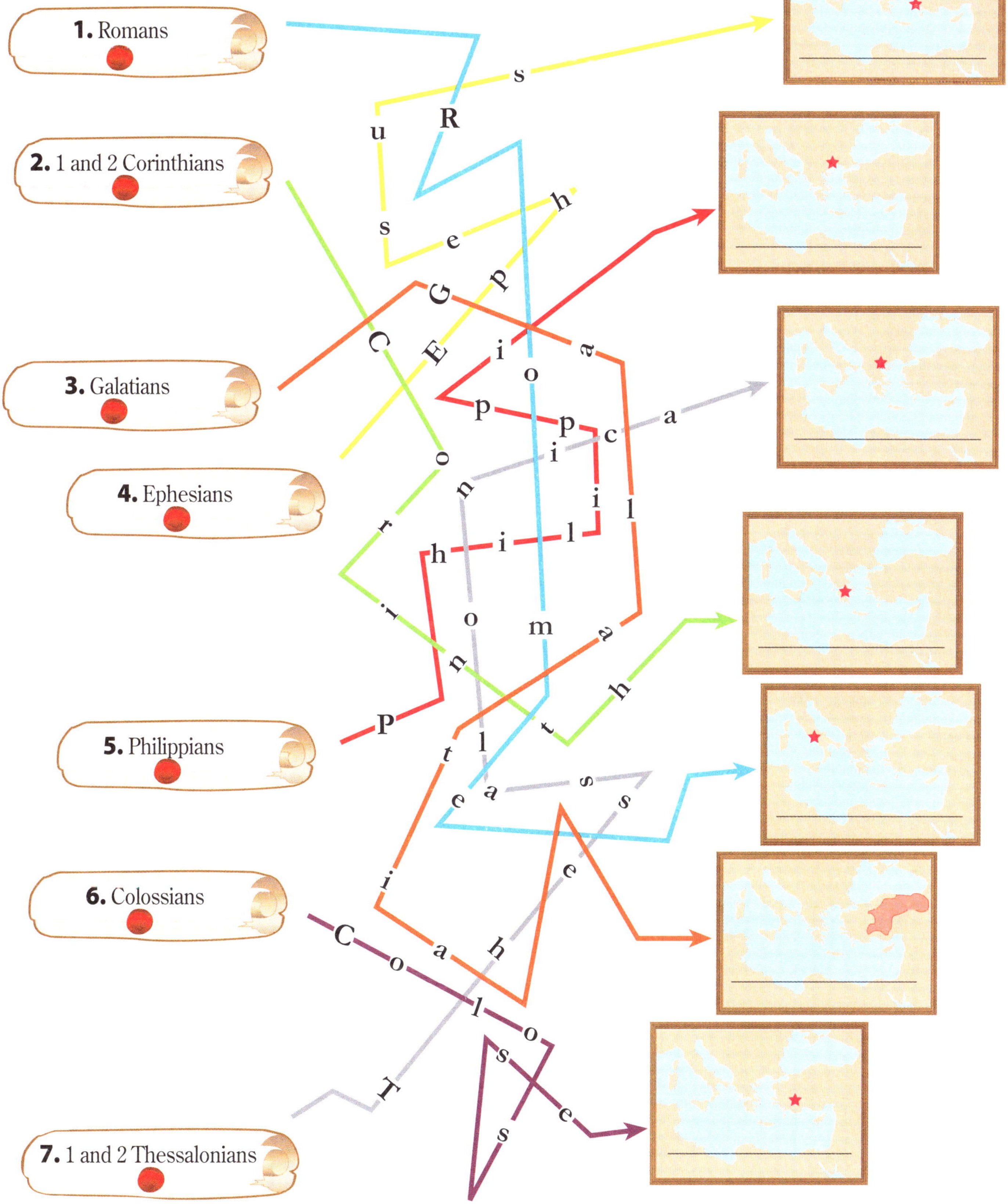

1. Romans _____
2. 1 and 2 Corinthians _____
3. Galatians _____
4. Ephesians _____
5. Philippians _____
6. Colossians _____
7. 1 and 2 Thessalonians _____

32.4 Paul's Journey to Rome

Read the following situation, and look up the verses. Circle the verses that can help David persevere to complete the task.

1. David erased his answer for the fourth time. He checked the numbers he had added, and they were still wrong! David thought, "It would be easier to have this problem marked wrong than to keep on trying."

Hebrews 11:1   Galatians 6:9

Psalm 121:2   1 Corinthians 8:3

2. Trace the stars with sentences that will help you persevere and finish well like Paul.

- God is pleased when I do my best.
- If I need help, I will ask.
- I will persevere on this job.
- I will work hard until I get the job done.
- God does not care if I finish my homework.
- I can do it.
- No one will help me.
- I will never finish this worksheet.
- My friends finished, so I should just stop.

Name _____

The Great Commission 33.1

1. Read the poem on the left about the Moravians. Use the example to help you write a poem about missions.

EXAMPLE

Moravians
caring, helpful
praying, obeying, going
bringing in the harvest
committed, bold
missionaries

_____
1 noun that states the topic

_____ _____
2 describing words

_____ _____ _____
3 action words

_____ _____ _____ _____
4 words in a phrase

_____ _____
2 describing words

_____
1 word to rename the topic

2. Read Psalm 2:8 and write a prayer about the harvest fields.

Dear God,

_____

_____

Amen

33.2 The Great Commission

Read the following statements. Draw the symbol that correctly shows what the person or people gave to help others learn about Jesus. Some statements may have more than one answer.

money   **talents**   **possessions**   **time**

1. Count Zinzendorf let persecuted believers live on his land.

2. The Moravians prayed 24 hours a day, seven days a week, for over 100 years.

3. Ida Scudder was a doctor in India for over 50 years.

4. A man gave Ida $10,000 to build a hospital for women in India.

5. Today, missionaries might teach English using the Bible.

6. Some believers make and sell things to fund mission projects around the world.

Write a way you can give each item to help others know about Jesus.

7. time _____

8. talents _____

9. possessions _____

10. money _____

Name _____

The Great Commission  33.3

Read the verses. Circle each reference that matches the word that tells what Jesus wants His followers to do.

1. **PRAY:** Matthew 9:38, Mark 1:38, Luke 10:2
2. **GIVE:** Matthew 10:42, Mark 9:41, John 1:5
3. **GO AND TELL:** Matthew 28:19, Mark 16:15, Luke 24:47, Acts 1:8

Answer the questions in complete sentences.

4. How might going and telling someone about Jesus change that person's life?

_____

_____

5. How might going and telling someone about Jesus change your life?

_____

_____

6. Write on the suitcase the names of several places God could ask you to go to and tell people about Jesus.

© Bible Grade 3

33.4 The Great Commission

1. Read this devotion written by Emma, age 10.

After reading Matthew 28:19, I decided to go out and be a witness for God. It all started when our class went to the Rescue Mission to help others. When I saw kids there, I really wanted to help. A few weeks later, my teacher told us about another ministry that also focused on witnessing to kids who do not have much. Then my mom and I thought, "Why not give the kids a special gift?" So we asked my class to collect candy, and my mom and I bought some cute bags and tons of candy! Most important, we put a Bible in each bag. Thanks to my class, we had 60 bags to give the kids at the ministry place! Helping other people made me so happy! That day God used me as a missionary!

What about you? Make plans to be a missionary by finishing the following sentences.

2. I can pray for _____.

3. I can give _____.

4. I can go to _____

and tell _____ about Jesus.

5. Use the code to explain the Great Commission.

Name _____

Review 34.1

Jesus taught so people could learn about God's plan of salvation and life in God's kingdom. Draw a matching line between each of Jesus' teachings and what Jesus wanted people to learn.

- heart attitudes that God blesses

1. parable •

2. Beatitudes •

3. "I am" statements •

4. The Lord's Prayer •

- a pattern to follow for talking with God

- an everyday story with a spiritual meaning

- word pictures to show that Jesus is divine

5. Write about one Bible truth Jesus taught and what you have learned from it.

_____

_____

_____

_____

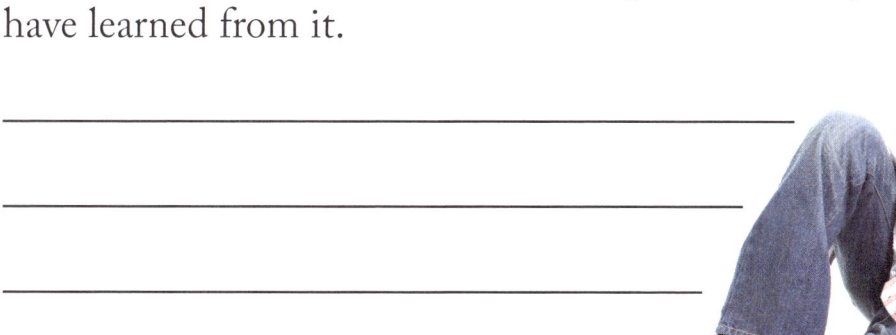

Bible Grade 3 — 133

34.2 Review

Choose one picture of a miracle from each row and answer the question in a complete sentence.

1. How did this miracle show that Jesus is God's Son?

   _____

   _____

   _____

   _____

   _____

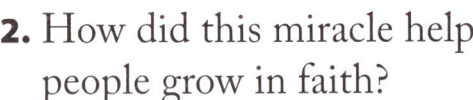

2. How did this miracle help people grow in faith?

   _____

   _____

   _____

   _____

3. How do Jesus' miracles help you believe in Jesus? _____

   _____

   _____

Name _____

Review 34.3

Through His selflessness, Jesus fulfilled God's plan of salvation. Write three words about how each period of Jesus' life helped fulfill God's plan. The first exercise has been done for you.

1. **Jesus came to the earth.**
   a. divine
   b. human
   c. relationship

2. **Jesus began His ministry.**
   a. _____
   b. _____
   c. _____

3. **Jesus called and equipped disciples.**
   a. _____
   b. _____
   c. _____

4. **Jesus died, rose again, and ascended.**
   a. _____
   b. _____
   c. _____

5. Write a sentence about what God's plan of salvation means for your life.

_____

_____

34.4 Review

After Jesus ascended to heaven, He sent the Holy Spirit. The good news of God's love flowed out from the early Church to the rest of the world. Circle the name that completes each sentence in the flow chart of events.

FLOW CHART

1. Because _____ listened to God and boldly preached at Pentecost, the early Church grew.

   Peter   Stephen   Paul

2. Because _____ died for his faith, the gospel spread out from Jerusalem.

   Luke   Stephen   Timothy

3. Because Jesus called to him on the road to Damascus, the apostle _____ became a great missionary.

   Paul   Stephen   Timothy

4. Because _____ was a missionary to the Gentiles, he wrote letters that became part of the New Testament.

   Stephen   Apollos   Paul

Finish the sentence.
5. Because I know the truth about God and His plan, I will

   _____
   _____
   _____
   _____
   _____
   _____.

Think about what you have learned this year and then complete the sentences.

6. I love and worship God more because _____
   _____.

7. My faith has grown because _____
   _____.

Glossary

beatitude a part of the Sermon on the Mount that teaches believers what their attitudes should be

believe to consider as true

blessed joyful

boldness having a confident willingness to meet danger and take risks

born again having accepted Jesus as Savior

citizen a person with rights to be protected by the government

compassion the act of seeing the suffering of others and being moved to action

conversion the time when a person decides to follow Jesus

courageous very brave even when afraid

divine being God or from God

endure remain faithful during hardship

equip provide what is needed for a certain purpose

evangelism the action of sharing the gospel

faithful consistently loyal and trustworthy

fellowship the sharing of similar experiences and friendship

focus total attention on something

forgiveness the letting go of a wrong without blame or demand for a penalty

fund to provide money for something

Glossary

glorify give honor and praise

gospel the good news of who Jesus is and what He did for people

grace something good given that is not earned

harvest a crop ready to be gathered

hospitality showing kindness and welcoming visitors

journey a trip from one place to another

martyr someone killed for their beliefs

mediator a go-between

ministry a job that is done in service to God and others

miracle an act of God that is impossible by human or natural causes

motive a reason for doing something

omnipotent all-powerful

omnipresent always present

omniscient all-knowing

parable an everyday story with a spiritual meaning

Pentecost the day God the Father sent the Holy Spirit to believers

persecution the cruel treatment of someone because of the person's beliefs

persevere to continue a task even when it is difficult

prayer talking with God

priority something deserving first attention

reap to gather a crop

Glossary

reconcile restore a relationship

repent feel sorry for something one has done and change one's action

respond react or answer

restore to return to its original condition

resurrection a return to life after having been dead

revelation an act of making truth known

riot a noisy disturbance caused by a crowd of people

salvation being saved from the punishment for sin and receiving eternal life

selfless having concern for others, not for oneself

sow to plant seeds for growth

spiritual blindness not being able to see truth about Jesus

spiritual sight the capability to see truth about Jesus

spiritual warfare an opportunity for believers to fight against evil with weapons that Jesus has provided

stewardship the careful and responsible management of possessions, abilities, and time

submission a state of having yielded to authority

synagogue a building in which Jewish people worship God

temptation an attempt to get someone to do something wrong

testimony an account given of something that happened

transfiguration a significant change

transform change remarkably

trustworthy worthy of trust, deserving of confidence

truth something that can never be proved false

witness tell others the gospel message

Bible Journal

Bible Journal

Bible Journal

Bible Journal

Bible Journal

Bible Journal

Bible Journal

Bible Journal

Bible Journal

Bible Journal

Bible Journal

Bible Journal

Bible Journal

Bible Journal

Bible Journal

Bible Journal